Macmillan Career Book

SOCIAL
WORKER

*Artist and Scientist
in Human Relations*

CAREER BOOK SERIES
Under Editorship of
Charles W. Cole

SOCIAL WORKER, by Margaret Williamson
CAREER DIPLOMAT, by Willard L. Beaulac
SCIENTIST, by Dr. Robert S. Morison
MINISTER, by John B. Coburn
PROFESSOR, by Fred B. Millett
LAWYER, by Talbot Smith
PHYSICIAN, by Dr. Dana W. Atchley
ARCHITECT, by Robert W. McLaughlin
NURSE, by Edith Patton Lewis
JOURNALIST, by Herbert Brucker

SOCIAL WORKER

*Artist and Scientist
in Human Relations*

by MARGARET WILLIAMSON

The Macmillan Company, New York
Collier-Macmillan Limited, London

Fourth Printing 1967

The Macmillan Company, New York
Collier-Macmillan Canada, Ltd., Toronto, Ontario

Library of Congress catalog card number: 63–16139

Printed in the United States of America

Foreword

It is an interesting fact that most young men who enter college planning to take a premedical course and to become physicians persevere in their intention. On the other hand, a great many college students who think that they are going to be engineers change their minds and shift toward some other vocation. Why should premedical students differ from preengineering students in the firmness of their intentions and decisions? A little investigation makes the answer to this question relatively clear.

The typical premedical student has a fairly well-defined notion of what a doctor really does. He has been to a doctor's office. He has been to a hospital either as a patient or as a visitor. He has read articles on the marvels of modern surgery and the new wonder drugs. In biology classes in secondary school, he has dissected frogs and rats. And the idea of healing people, even by complex techniques, is not hard to understand.

The normal preengineering student, on the other hand, has only the vaguest understanding of what the work of an engineer is really like. Perhaps he thinks of it as mainly building bridges. He has no conception of the differences among chemical engineering, civil engineering, and aeronautical engineering. Nor does he realize that the most rigorous training in basic science and mathematics is part of the necessary equipment for an engineer. When, in college, he comes to a really difficult course such as differential equations, he may suddenly discover that his aptitudes are more limited and his tastes less mathematical than he had thought. He reassesses his earlier decision and alters his career plan, but often with some lost motion and an impairment of his motivation.

There can be little doubt that young people today have a much more difficult time in trying to decide on a vocation than did their predecessors a generation ago. For this situation, several reasons can be found.

In the first place, because our society has grown so complex, there are many more callings and professions than there used to be. One has only to think of new kinds of jobs such as airport traffic manager, physical therapist, digital-computer programmer, or television repairman to realize the truth of this statement. In addition, many professions have been broken down into specialties. A tax lawyer may never plead a case in court; an insurance broker may handle nothing but casualty problems; a plastic surgeon may never perform an appendectomy.

In the second place, many callings now require such a prolonged and expensive preparation that a young person instinctively tries hard not to make a mistake that may mean wasted years and money. To become a practicing physician requires about ten years of college, medical school, and internship. A nurse normally has two or more years in college in addition to nursing school. Many teachers, even in the primary grades, have graduate as well as bachelor's degrees.

Finally, this is an introspective age. Young people are given all sorts of psychological, vocational, and aptitude tests. They are given counseling and guidance. Their parents and teachers worry about their adjustment to society, to school, to peer groups. College students today keep asking themselves, "Who am I?"—a question rarely, if ever, considered by their predecessors before World War II. Part of that question, of course, has to be answered by a young man or woman who is seeking to choose a profession, for such a choice depends on personal abilities, tastes, and ideals, as well as on motivation.

The series of Career Books that Macmillan is publishing is specifically designed to help young people make the difficult vocational decisions that confront them. Each volume is written by a distinguished expert in the field who has had long years of practice in the career in question. It seeks to explain the nature of the profession, the qualities needed for it, the methods of entering it, the preparation required for it, the rewards it offers, the hazards and difficulties it presents. Each author tries to do even a little more: to give the reader a feeling of what it is like to be an architect, a professor, or a social worker.

This volume is one of the most interesting in the series, for it deals with a field of activity that only in the last thirty years or so has become truly a profession. But the author points out that this transition has now taken place and that the best opportunities for service and advancement in social work come today to those who are, in fact, professionals and who have behind them appropriate professional education. Another factor that makes this book important is that, while more and more men are going into social work, it is one of the professions in which women have made outstanding contributions and still have special opportunities.

While the author describes clearly and factually the economic picture for social workers, the kind of preparation needed, and the many opportunities that are open because the demand for trained professionals grows even faster than the supply, she also goes further. Her own ideals imbue the work, and she depicts her profession as one peculiarly appropriate for those who want to be of service and who can derive lasting satisfaction from helping people.

Margaret Williamson is especially well qualified to write an authoritative volume on social work. Born in North Wales, she received her bachelor's degree from Girton College of Cambridge University. She then came to the United States and took an M.A. at Columbia University. For thirty-eight years, she worked for the Y.W.C.A., first in its employment service in New York City and then on the staff of its National Board. For the Board, she engaged in field travel, administered a program department, and served as Director of the Training Department.

Miss Williamson was for eleven years a full-time member of the New York School of Social Work (now the Columbia University School of Social Work). She has recently been teaching also at the Graduate School of Social Work at Rutgers.

Santiago, Chile   CHARLES W. COLE
April, 1964

Contents

1

A Young Profession
with Roots
in the Past

When we think of a trained social worker today, we are thinking of a member of a profession that, in company with such other professions as medicine and law, is devoted to helping people with their basic needs and problems in living; indeed, these professions are often referred to as "helping professions."

Along with other important elements that go into the making of such a profession are the requirements that its underlying wisdom and insights rest on carefully selected and organized areas of knowledge, and that its services to people be given in ways that are scientifically determined, constantly tested in practice, and continuously revised as new knowledge emerges.

If considered solely in these terms, social work must be called a "young" profession, since the organization of its particular areas of knowledge and the testing of methods for putting that knowledge to work in serving people are of relatively recent date.

Yet the roots of this profession lie deep in the age-old impulses of man to befriend his neighbor and to help him in practical ways when he is caught in situations that threaten his well-being.

Social Work
and the American Tradition

In this country, these impulses toward friendly helpfulness were strengthened and supported by the democratic ideas which the builders of a virile new society brought to bear on their common life as a nation in the New World.

This suggests that the philosophy, basic principles, and methods of social work today will take on additional depth and meaning, and a certain irresistible logic and color, if they are studied against a background of the ideas and beliefs that went into the creation of our American state.

What are these dominant ideas, where did they come from, and in what ways has social work responded to their influence?

The earliest settlers in this country did not bring with them clearly defined notions about what would make a democratic society; they had never lived in one. From their own frequently hard life experiences in the Old World, however, they did bring strong feelings of resistance to any controls that tended to violate the personal selfhood of the individual man.

Those of Judaic or Christian religious heritage brought with them their churches' teachings about the dignity and worth of man as a child of God and about their obligation, in the name of their faith, to care for the sick and needy, the homeless, deserted, and handicapped.

In Europe, meanwhile, the winds of a new and more liberal way of thinking about man and his destiny had risen above a whisper; it began to be taken more for granted that man's freedom, his dignity, well-being, and happiness counted importantly; that, indeed, as an ancient Greek philosopher had put it, "Man is the measure of all things." "Wonders are many," wrote Sophocles, "and none is more wonderful than man." Many people who reached these shores showed the influence of this way of thinking in strongly humanistic attitudes toward their fellows and in ready assumption of the responsibility to increase their well-being.

It would be a mistake to assume that these basic ideas about the essential rights of the individual and the responsibility for assuring him help, as he needed it, reached full expression as a way of life in the early days of the Republic. Indeed, their full accomplishment is not yet in sight.

But the Direction Was Unmistakable

It was under the strong influence of these ways of thinking about the individual man that those responsible set down in bold, clear strokes the imperatives of a democratic constitution. Read again Thomas Jefferson's Preamble to the Declaration of Independence and you will be able to trace the unmistakable influence of exponents of seventeenth-century English liberalism and of Rousseau's declarations for humanism and equalitarianism in eighteenth-century France.

The effect on the builders of a brave new democracy in the West went deep. The individual and his rights stood at the center of their pronouncements, and, in political terms, the consent of the governed and such essential freedoms as those of assembly, speech, and religion were proclaimed as basic. It was not difficult to see behind these specific statements the emergence of philosophical ideas that emphasized social equality, the necessity for equal opportunity for all, and the obligation to resist all forms of injustice wherever they appeared in social arrangements.

It is within the rich promise of these principles that the heritage of present-day social work should be sought, rather than in their frequently faulty expression through the years by persons whose tendencies to blame and punish people needing help, to discriminate in the giving of service, and to turn a deaf ear to flagrant injustice gave the lie to the basic principles underlying the attempt to realize a true democracy.

Social work today presents, as one of its strongest appeals to the career seeker, its central and persistent dedication to the realization, in fact, of the "American dream." Underlying this dream is equality of opportunity for physical, social, and emotional well-being, as well as the assurance to every individual of just dealing and essential freedom.

The modern case worker, sensitively helping a bewildered young widow to draw together the torn pieces of her life, is within our finest tradition when she sees her client first—and all the time—as a person in her own right; with this image clearly before her, the case worker will move the more surely to help her client realize her capacity to act on her own behalf and to use, with dignity and self-respect, the counseling help the worker is equipped to give.

For example, the case worker and her client will have to make some immediate decisions after a careful joint estimate of the extent of existing resources. Where can the young woman live and make a home for her little girl? Is finding a job desirable or feasible? To what extent will a concerned government's program of aid to dependent children expand her resources? Planning for a life ahead when a familiar pattern has been shattered will bring its own emotional burdens; but the experience of making step-by-step decisions, with the help of a worker who cares, will emphasize that it is *her* life that is being planned, that the decisions are *hers* to make, and that the resources opened up by the worker are *hers* by rightful heritage as a person.

The group worker in the settlement house or community center is at work in the same tradition when, seeing his club of nine-year-olds as persons and citizens-to-be, he applies imaginative effort to fostering in their group life democratic ways of self-government and consideration for the rights of others. At the same time he will be drawing from the resources of his agency and its community those facilities which will help to assure to otherwise deprived children of a city's streets equal opportunity for happy play, sturdy growth, and creative self-expression.

Such illustrations could be multiplied almost indefinitely. The nature of the problem or need will vary from situation to situation, but each one will point up an essential truth: social work is intimately concerned with people, their needs and problems, their essential rights as individuals, and their own capacities for solving their problems.

A few more signposts from the past are in order now to point toward the content of the rest of the book. In succeeding chapters we shall see social work and social workers as they are today; the nature of the problems they deal with; what they actually do; what it takes to do it; and how to get ready in college and professional school to undertake these responsibilities. Social work as a career opportunity, its actual fields of practice, the rewards and frustrations that can be expected, and some view of what the future holds for this young, vigorous, and rapidly growing profession will be considered.

The society within which the American state came into being was largely agricultural and relatively simple in structure. People were not crowded together. The relative self-sufficiency of families emphasized independence and self-resourcefulness. The problems that might arise when people lived more closely together were scarcely glimpsed. Response by men and women to situations of human need was expressed in simple acts of charity, very much as had been true in Colonial times.

This, however, was not to remain the pattern for very long. Rapid growth in population, greater diversity in its makeup, and shifts in the economic outlook of the country, through its industrial development, brought great changes to the American people. With greater concentration of population in growing industrial centers, more people faced new and more complicated problems. New and different forms of help were needed. The pressures called for more *organized* ways of helping; and before the end of the nineteenth century, voluntary organizations and welfare institutions of various kinds, often under church or religiously motivated group sponsorship, had come into being. Those responsible for organizing and maintaining the services of many of these early programs were largely volunteers. These men and women worked untiringly and with a sense of deep compassion for those in trouble or need. Modern social work owes much to their spirit of dedication, their unwavering acceptance of responsibility, and their ingenuity in making and carrying out plans.

Many of the older social, educational, and welfare organizations now carrying on extensive programs in this country had their beginnings in this period. In the governmental field, state boards of public charities and boards for the oversight of public institutions for children, and the disabled, and of prisons began to appear.

At the same time, private organizations multiplied to meet a variety of human needs. Groups interested in the alleviation of problems rising chiefly from poverty drew together into associated charities or charity organization societies— forerunners of today's family service agencies. The YMCA and the YWCA expanded their services in this period, and in the emergence of the Young Men's Hebrew Association we had the beginnings of what is usually known today as the Jewish Community Center.

The period was marked, too, by the beginning of the settlement movement in America. A major approach to community problems—to a large extent continuing today—was the actual residence in the settlement house of workers, paid and volunteer, who assumed an active neighbor role in a geographically defined community, a community seen as one of neighbors bound together for mutual helpfulness and creative development.

It was not wholly surprising that, under the influence of the strongly individualistic ideas that directed our government, the early organized efforts for giving help frequently showed a similar individualistic approach and attitude of mind toward those needing help—ideas that were later to undergo change.

The logic of the thinking of that period was rather simple: the government gave assurance to every individual citizen of certain basic rights and freedoms; he was a citizen of a wonderful new nation, and it was expected that his own untrammeled initiative, thrift, and "right" living would enable him to live and prosper and reap the full rewards of his individual citizenship. It followed, in this reasoning, that if an individual fell into difficulties that made it impossible for him to get along without outside help, it was more than likely his own fault. How to reform the individual, and lead him to change his ways, was often a major concern of those organized to give help.

This view did not necessarily lessen the compassion with which help was given, but it did result in a lack of consideration for the individual's own ability to help with his problem, and it led to an accompanying pattern, therefore, of "doing for" or "doing to" rather than "doing with." It was not until the time when Jane Addams founded Hull-House in Chicago in 1889 that a new principle emerged, namely, that "one does good, if at all, *with* people, not *to* people." This continues to be the approach of social work today.

The focus on the individual and the tendency to place on him the blame for the unfortunate circumstances in which he found himself served, too, as a sort of blinder to keep would-be helpers from recognizing such causes of distress as the rapid influx into crowded cities of thousands of bewildered people, to many of whom American ways were alien and threatening. Between 1780 and 1860 our population increased from 2,781,000 to 31,443,321.

Here were situations that hurt not only individuals, but whole groups. Men and women both inside and outside the existing organizations began to ask whether the old ways of helping were adequate or just.

With a sense of having failed to invoke fully that principle of the democratic faith that "men are created equal" and endowed with "inalienable rights" to "life, liberty, and the pursuit of happiness," leaders in movements for social reform turned their attention to the government itself. What responsibility for human welfare might rest in its legislative chambers and halls of justice?

It became clear that while the Constitution had placed the individual in a central position politically, it was not devised to help him directly in the complexities of his everyday living. A view had persisted that man would fare better without government "interference" in these areas of his life; that, in fact, the best government was the least government.

During this period of rapid industrial growth—approximately from 1860 to 1900—the government's attention was devoted largely to technological and economic advances and to the legal protection of private enterprise. That this should result in a tacit favoring, by government, of a relatively smaller, economically wealthy class while often disregarding the needs of large numbers of people—often dispossessed by the workings of the economy itself—had not been foreseen by the founding fathers. As it became clearer, however, that property rights had assumed preeminence over basic human rights, there was increasing evidence of an aroused public conscience. Pressure became stronger for new interpretations of the role of government and for procedures that would more nearly achieve a government of all the people working in the interest of all.

A significant place in this struggle for needed reforms on behalf of the common man was taken by the country's writers; following the more philosophical approach of Edward Bellamy's *Looking Backward 2000–1887*, published in 1888, there came more focused and more caustic attacks on the social evils of the day from the pens of such journalists as Jacob Riis, on New York City's slums; John Spargo, on the evils of child labor; Ida Tarbell, on the corrupt methods of the big oil combines; and Lincoln Steffens, on political corruption and the evils of the political machine.

By the turn of the century, and in the period immediately before the First World War, social workers, busy with the day-to-day programs of their organizations, were also giving leadership in many areas of social reform. The tireless and courageous efforts of such leaders as Jane Addams, battling for human rights on many fronts, marked the passing of an era when simple charity was considered enough. The new era called for reform, through legislative means, of factors in the environment that could only result in human suffering.

In 1910, as president of the National Conference of Charities and Corrections, Miss Addams deplored social work's slowness in recognizing the relationship of poverty to modern industrialism. She summoned its workers to a new vision of their profession as an integral part of the larger social movement that, to reach its ultimate goals, must engage in social action. Associated with this new way of thinking in social work was the leadership of such men as Owen R. Lovejoy, who headed a group that made a significant study of standards of living and labor (1912), and Edward T. Devine, who wrote on what the role of social work should be in relation to political parties in this country.

Social Work Today

From this shift in thinking has come one of the most important guiding beliefs of present-day social work: a person's individual problems are usually interwoven with those that affect society as a whole, and healthier living conditions, greater economic security, and sounder relations between groups of differing racial or religious background will go far in helping an individual with his own growth and adjustment problems.

While depressions and the aftermaths of war dramatized the need for expanded programs of health and welfare, it was not until well along in the twentieth century that state and federal governments began to assume a major role in them. This slowness was undoubtedly due to conflicts in thinking, even among those with humanitarian concerns. On the one hand, there were, and still are, fears that to expand government's involvement in human welfare might endanger individual freedom; on the other hand, there was the conviction that the needs of people in a rapidly growing industrial society could no longer be met adequately through the "one-by-one" approach of private philanthropy.

Most social workers today believe that this is not necessarily a "never the twain shall meet" situation and that social work, strongly influenced by both philosophies, has a contribution to make in bringing together the two approaches, using in its everyday practice the essential truths of both points of view.

The lineal descendant of the "friendly visitor" of an earlier day is the modern case worker working intimately with individuals and their families and bringing to bear on his service new knowledge drawn from psychiatry and the social sciences. This deepening understanding of how individual situations of stress affect the capacities of people to get along provides essential knowledge on which to base legislative action and large-scale government plans for human welfare. In turn, emphasis on the importance of environment and experience in tackling human problems on a broad scale enhances the social worker's ability to understand the problems of his individual client. He has assurance, too, that the resources of the government's programs for social security will be available to meet the basic health and welfare needs of his clients.

A further discovery that has exerted a strong influence on modern social work is that not all the problems that harass individuals and families are due to economic breakdown and dependency. New conditions of living in crowded communities brought great problems in human relations and in adaptation to an intensely speeded-up rate of social change. There is a certain triteness in the reminder that man does not live by bread alone; yet here is a fact to be dealt with soundly and sensitively in the person-to-person and in the more intimate group services, as well as in the broadly based mass programs.

As we move into the succeeding chapters of this book,

we might look at social work with Dr. Nathan Cohen as having from its past, "found a methodology and a two-pronged approach growing out of the two types of humanitarian influence. The 'two-pronged' approach includes concern, on the one hand, for the adjustment and development of the individual toward more satisfying human relations and, on the other, for improving the social institutions within which the individual functions. It seeks through its work with individuals, groups and the community to help people find within themselves the resources for solving both the problems that affect them alone and those that affect people in general. Thus it is concerned not only with the individual and the social institutions within which he functions but also with the relationship between these two factors." *

The terms "individuals," "groups," and "community" in this quotation suggest particular methods of practice that have come to characterize social work today when we speak of case work, group work, and community organization; fuller descriptions of each of these areas and methods of practice will come in succeeding pages. Meanwhile, in the next chapter, we shall take a look at some of the varieties of human problems and pressing needs that challenge all present-day social workers, whatever their particular area of practice.

* Nathan E. Cohen, *Social Work in the American Tradition*, The Dryden Press, Inc., New York, 1958. Quoted by permission of Holt, Rinehart and Winston, Inc.

2

Where Problems in Living Press Hard

Social work begins with concern for people:

Concern for their well-being and with all that threatens it, whether spelled out in the starkness of corroding poverty or in the breakdown or slow recovery of physical or mental health;

Concern for the ambitions and hopes of people that go down to defeat in the ugly realities of crowded and inadequate homes; in filthy crime-ridden streets, where racial conflicts flare into ugly violence; and in the debasing experience of discrimination and the violation of human dignity that comes with relegation to second-class citizenship;

Concern for those who have sought and tried antisocial or unlawful ways of solving their problems, often resulting in arrest and sentence under the law;

Concern for the restoration to useful activity and dignity of those whose physical or mental disabilities have caused them to be pushed aside;

Concern for the nation's children everywhere, for their safety and their overwhelming need for loving and understanding care, lest their "young souls be smothered

out before they do quaint deeds and fully flaunt their
pride"; *

Concern for the bewilderment of teen-agers trying to stake
out a meaningful place in a seemingly nonaccepting,
shifting, and untrustworthy world and for all young people in the throes of making choices in matters of school-
ing, jobs, family relationships, sex, and marriage;

And deep concern for older men and women who feel
lonely, unwanted, and stripped of dignity because they
are nonproducers in a society that puts a high premium
on productivity, yet denies to so many the opportunity
for achieving it.

The areas of problem and need with which social work is
concerned today are not, at first glance, very different from
those of fifty years ago. A careful look, however, reveals differences in the nature and intensity of given problems under
the impact of changed social conditions. Differences show
up, too, in the ways that solutions are being sought by those
experiencing the problem and by those seeking to help them.

These are among the major areas of distress with which
social workers deal today. Some of them present problems
that persist from the past; others take on new forms or intensity under the pressures of modern social conditions.

Poverty

Poverty was the first and the most crucial of all human
problems to be recognized, and the earliest forms of organized help were to aid the needy. In a wealthy country, with
an extraordinarily high standard of living, poverty still holds
many thousands of American families in its rigid and frightening clutches:

When Mrs. Wilcox's husband died, her problems seemed overwhelming to her. Frightened and feeling very much alone, she

* Vachel Lindsay, "The Leaden-Eyed," *Collected Poems,* The Macmillan
Company, New York, 1925.

had not known where to turn until her pastor referred her to the county welfare office. Here, sensitive questioning uncovered a situation of desperate financial need for which immediate relief was imperative. Mrs. Wilcox needed help in making application for the financial assistance to which she and her children were entitled and which would help make it possible for her to hold her young family together.

In an earlier day, Mrs. Wilcox might still have turned to her pastor, but his resources for helping would have been limited to small emergency "tiding-over" church funds for charitable purposes or his own scanty personal reserves.

Helping those eligible obtain needed financial aid may be only a first step, however; poverty, characteristically, brings many other problems in its train, particularly in areas of family breakdown.

Unemployment

Unemployment is a major cause of poverty, and many people become unemployed through no fault of their own. Industries and businesses fold up or move away; mechanical devices replace manual skills and reduce the need for manpower. Whatever the cause, extended unemployment brings stresses that go beyond the need for immediate financial assistance:

> *Mr. Seeley has lost confidence in himself* through continued unemployment. In common with many people, he finds it difficult to ask for help; to do so seems an admission of inability to make a living and to support a family. "And what will people think?"

Encouragement to take a new look at his situation, to get a view of it that is more realistic than a blocking sense of personal failure, and knowledgeable referral to community resources, such as the U.S. Employment Service, for turning up a job may be enough to start Mr. Seeley on his way again with renewed courage and self-respect.

But Mr. Cooper and his family will need more extended help. Difficulty in getting along with his employer or fellow workers and inertia or confusion about his role as a worker have led to repeated periods of unemployment. Relationships in Mr. Cooper's family are seriously deteriorating under his constant bickering with his wife and children.

To help him understand why he loses jobs may not be easy, and Mr. Cooper may not be immediately able to use the counseling assistance offered by a social worker. The effort to help him understand must go steadily on, however, while more immediate planning is undertaken with the family to solve related problems that have begun to undermine its stability.

It may be that help in budgeting her limited financial resources, in securing overdue medical or dental care, or in enabling one or more of the children to get away to summer camp will serve to lessen Mrs. Cooper's feelings of hopelessness and give new impetus to her efforts on behalf of her family.

Health Problems

Physical or mental health breakdown may bring problems of peculiar difficulty and poignancy:

Mr. Rowe needs somebody to stand by while he takes the hard steps needed to place his wife in a state mental hospital. The "standing by" may start with a period when Mr. Rowe will need help in accepting the necessity for his wife's hospitalization and in understanding what kind of care and treatment is to be expected. A family pattern is disrupted here; the services of a visiting homemaker may be needed. Mr. Rowe has to be helped to find the courage to face a new way of life for himself and his children and to recognize some of the possible means of satisfaction in that new life.

Mr. Brown has just learned that he has tuberculosis, and the social service department of his hospital is alerted to help him and his family plan for the time it will take for him to get well again. Extended absence from the family, loss of employment, and deep fears—his own and his family's—will need to be taken into account. Warm individual and family counseling must go into a program of service to Mr. Brown as he sets out on what may be a long road back to health.

Youth in Trouble

Many young people find themselves in what seems to them "no-way-out" situations. Frightened and lonely, they need help, not only in finding constructive solutions for the immediate problem, but in rebuilding courage, self-respect, and trust in their own capacity to direct their lives and handle their own problems.

Eighteen-year-old Diana G.—unmarried—is going to have a baby. This is not the usual happy occasion for greeting a new member of society; Diana's baby will be born without a father's name to go on the register. Perhaps bitter, and probably deeply frightened, Diana finds it difficult to deal with the decisions that have to be made. Where can she go to await the baby's birth? Shall she keep her baby or release it for adoption? If she keeps it, how can she care for it? Her family, preoccupied with their own shock and anger, as well as with fears of disclosure, is not helping much at the moment, and Diana feels lost and alone with her trouble. In the planning that will be needed, skillful help will be directed toward enabling Diana to rally her own resources of courage and wisdom to find a solution for a future that will be the best—the most constructive—for both her and her baby.

Louis is seventeen, homeless, and unemployed; he has been using drugs for nearly two years, and now he is in court for rifling cars and apartments in his desperate need for money to finance his habit. In the hope that rehabilitation may be possible, the court assigns him for probation. A probation officer, who is a trained social worker, becomes Louis' friend, sees him regularly, and taps the community's resources in his behalf. This may mean planning for medical treatment, a place to live and a job, and a place to play and make friends; most important of all, this worker may be the first human being Louis has ever been able to trust in what has been to him a largely untrustworthy and vindictive world. Compassion, respect, and infinite patience will be needed, and Louis' situation may not be immediately solvable. There is real sickness here: the effects of drug addiction go very deep; most communities are woefully lacking in treatment facilities, and return to the habit is unhappily very frequent. This social worker must carry a dual responsibility: to the sick boy and to a community that may suffer through his behavior. Surveillance for the court is a necessary part of the job; when this is combined with warm friendliness and sensitive counseling aimed at helping Louis find strengths within himself to make the decisions that are his to make and to change his attitudes and ways of behaving, the case may come to a successful close.

"Is this for us?" Two little girls who had gazed, wide-eyed, at gaily colored posters outside a YWCA building describing exciting camp activities advanced timidly into the lobby and up to the reception desk. Their question told a vivid story of lives—short as theirs were—that had been cramped by the bitter experience of exclusion, of always being made to feel different, of never being quite sure how white people were going to act toward you.

In the nature of things, social work and social workers are constantly involved in situations of racial discrimination and conflict. Committed as they are to giving service without regard to differences in color or creed, they will be found working shoulder to shoulder with all those who are seeking to broaden the application of equal opportunity for all, to resist discriminatory practices wherever they appear and to break down the barriers of distrust and hatred that keep people apart. They will use every opportunity for helping people, their clientele included, to accept and respect difference and to learn to get along with people who are different from themselves.

Most of the Warriors—dropouts from school—are without jobs. This means "no money" in a money-conscious society and, therefore, deprivation in relation to things to do and places to go that are taken for granted by other fifteen- to eighteen-year-olds in our society. The contrasting actualities are very sharp—nothing to do; no place to play; nowhere to take a girl; no fun. Their crowded homes send them into the streets, where they gather as a gang on empty lots or hang around corner candy stores or shoe-cleaning shops. Unfamiliar faces and strange tongues are becoming a part of their neighborhood, and as these newcomers begin to move in groups, they look like rivals to the Warriors; fear mounts as to whether they can hold on to the pitiful street "territories" they have staked out as their own. Incidents of intergroup violence break out, and as tensions rise, outlets are sought in acts of vandalism in the neighborhood that bring terror to its residents. Fear of physical danger or the psychological need to belong brings other boys—frequently younger ones—into the gang; individually they are often without heart for many of the group's activities, but the need for the security the gang affords keeps them in. Fear and suspicion are dominant feelings; ignorance of its purposes and disbelief in the sincerity of its leadership keep them out of the community center, although there may be wistful yearnings for its gym or games room.

Since they will not come in under their own steam, can the center move out to them? The Warriors are cagy and nonresponsive to outsiders, seeing them as "know-nothings" or "do-gooders" or in some vague way as representative of a society that has its hand against them and their kind and makes no place for them for either work or play.

Making contact in the first place, standing by when the group is in trouble, helping with individual needs for jobs or medical care, or dealing with emergency situations—often involving entire families—may be part of the social worker's efforts to build confidence and gain acceptance. It will all take a long time; always, too, there will be the possibility that a tenuous relationship will be broken by immediately uncontrollable episodes of gang violence, and the long, slow process will have to start again.

Neglected Children

No pages in the story of human problems and needs stir a deeper sense of compassion and urgency than those describing situations that call out for active intervention to safeguard the welfare of the most innocent of society's victims —and its most precious possession—its children:

Nine-year-old Susie is a "latchkey kid"; her mother is one of the twenty per cent of all mothers with children under eighteen who work for wages outside the home. Susie has a key. After school, it opens a door to a home without a mother in it, to loneliness, and to too many opportunities for what her mother calls "badness." Frequent forays on her mother's tiny cache of nickels and dimes have brought Susie hard cuffs if not severe beatings; truancy from school and petty pilfering from neighborhood stores have come to the attention of her teacher. Whether "up to no good" in her empty home or ranging the streets with other latchkey kids, Susie is in real trouble.

If the effects of neglect and being too much on her own have gone deep, the skills of a child welfare worker, working with Susie and her mother over a long period of time, may be needed to straighten things out. Perhaps part of the answer may be found in the neighborhood settlement house, where, with the help of another social worker, Susie can find her way, along with others her age, into exciting new experiences of "doing things and going places." With a chance to give as well as take—and to feel the warmth of belonging and of being wanted—Susie's old rebellious feelings that made her a "problem" may gradually disappear.

Audrey Jean is three: a roly-poly little girl with curls; but from time to time there are glints of fear and bewilderment in her dark eyes as she moves with the other children along the corridors of the city's temporary shelter. Something important is missing; the people here are kind, but missing is a special kind of feeling that Audrey Jean cannot quite describe—and sometimes it hurts more when you can't explain about things. Audrey Jean's missing has to do with the no-longer-felt arms that held her when her mother picked her up each afternoon at the day-care center and with the softness of a no-longer-heard voice calling her name; but Audrey Jean's mother has been killed in an accident on her way to work, and there is nobody to take her place. Audrey Jean doesn't remember her father; he left them quite a while ago, and his whereabouts are unknown.

What can be done for Audrey Jean? Careful exploration of a potential foster home for the child; perhaps interviewing possible adoptive parents, in a serious and determined quest for just the right kind of home for the particular needs of a particular little girl; and all through this process, with its legal and other kinds of involvements, there must be time to be with Audrey Jean herself, learning more about her from being with her, helping her know she is cared for, encouraging her in needed play, and if and when plans work out for a new home, helping her get ready for the new experience.

At the Other End of the Age Scale

In an age classification, Mr. Franz would be counted in the "over 70" column; but to understand Mr. Franz's problems, generalizations and categorizing would have to stop right there!

Mr. Franz was born in Europe and came to this country nearly fifty years ago. His skillful hands had taken him quickly into steady employment in a woodworking shop. Marriage and the birth of a son rounded out his immediate world with happiness, and his rich baritone voice rang out at home and in the shop in the old-country songs he had learned as a boy.

Trouble started for Mr. Franz when a machine was brought into the shop that did his work more quickly and with less cost. For a time, he was kept on doing things that gnawed at his pride; the songs disappeared, and more and more frequent outbursts of temper brought shrugged shoulders as his boss and fellow workers turned away from him. Mr. Franz felt isolated and rebuffed and without means for reinstating him-

self. Unemployed finally, Mr. Franz entered a bewildering
period of job-hunting. It was hard for him to accept the changes
he found—no shops of the kind he had known; no demand
for his particular skills; and when it became a situation of "any
job at all," he found frightening the increasingly frequent response: "We need a younger man," or, "You're too old for our
needs here." Less and less employable in the open job market,
his savings dwindled, and loss of self-respect weighed on him
heavily.

During his wife's long illness, all savings disappeared; and at
the time of her death, Mr. Franz became almost wholly dependent on his son—not an easy situation for the son, already
responsible for a family of five.

A tiny room off the kitchen in his son's apartment was an immediate solution, but difficulties soon began to arise. Mr. Franz
had no friends in the neighborhood and did not get out much;
the apartment was crowded, mealtimes confused, and the
clamor of the children bothersome. They grew weary of his
long and involved stories from the past; they didn't like his
songs, and he didn't like theirs. There were clashes with his
daughter-in-law over the children's behavior and over his criti-
cism of her handling of it. His dire warnings that they "would
all come to a bad end" were not appreciated. As far as his
daughter-in-law was concerned, he was "always underfoot,"
"untidy," and "interfering" in matters that didn't concern him.
His son's weary, "Can't you be a bit more cooperative, Pop?"
only served to line him up on the other side—a disloyal son.
Faced finally with an ultimatum from his wife—"Either he
goes or I do"—the son sought help from a family agency.

There is much to be done here, and a worker begins to
help the family's dramatis personae singly and as a group;
there will be efforts to untangle the snarled relationships and
to reduce the tensions that get in the way of an objective
look at the situation and their combined resources for dealing with it. What are the limits of financial capacity? Are
any adjustments in the physical arrangements of the apartment possible? Can a room be found and maintained in Mr.
Franz's old neighborhood, where he knows more people?
What groups in the new or the old neighborhood can help

Mr. Franz find friends and interests outside the home to fill empty hours and give him some measure of the status as a person and the response from people he so sorely needs?

Perhaps some teamwork may enter here. Perhaps a social worker from a neighborhood center helps Mr. Franz find a satisfying place in a group of his own age—and what assets he brings: the glee club gets a new voice and the craft shop a skilled craftsman. A success story? Yes, but it happens all the time!

These are no more than thumbnail sketches of people and groups in trouble or need; inevitably, they present an incomplete picture. Areas of human problems are vast; and even within one situation, the needs may be multiple and very demanding. Taken together, they suggest that some situations will require social work activities on behalf of individuals or groups that are largely preventive and protective. In others, an individual or family situation is the crucial one—whether it is for financial aid to maintain life itself, planning for hospital care, standing by a lonely boy or girl who must make decisions that will seriously affect an already precarious future, intervening on behalf of a helpless child who could be maimed emotionally, or finding the makings of a better way of life for a lonely old man or woman. Still other situations require determined efforts to change social conditions that inevitably breed social problems—overcrowded homes and schools; unstandardized working conditions; inadequate provisions for medical care or recreation; racial discrimination in housing, in jobs, or in use of the community's resources for rest and play.

Then what really is the role of social work in society today? How does its role determine the goals toward which its workers will direct all their efforts, whatever the situation? Why does this role obligate them to the mastery and disciplined use of the knowledge and skills of their profession?

Before moving to the next chapter, and a closer look at

social work as a profession, it may help to ponder a simple statement that suggests some answers to these questions:

"Social work is work *with* and *for* people. It is a helping profession. Its purpose is to help troubled people cope with problems that arise in their relationships to each other and to the world in which they live—problems that frequently stand in the way of productive and satisfying living.

"Some of these problems are as old as human history. Others are the product of the tensions of our times. Some have their roots in unwholesome community and social conditions. Others are the outgrowth of personality disorders. But most of the problems with which social workers deal are the combined product of environmental stress and inner emotional strain, the one interacting on the other." *

* From the pamphlet *Social Work as a Profession,* issued by the Council on Social Work Education, 345 East 46th Street, New York 17, N.Y.

3

Social Work as a Profession

The preceding chapter gave glimpses of some of the baffling human problems that call for the knowledge and skills of the trained social worker. People differ in their ways of meeting trouble and in their capacity to deal with it constructively. A first feeling may be of stark desperation or a need to lash out at others as the "causes" of their distress. Withdrawal from individual responsibility or attachment to wholly unrealistic "ways out" will as often slow up the efforts to help as constructive cooperation will expedite them. There will be feelings of fear and hurt, hopelessness and loss of self-esteem, as well as eagerness to find the best solution; all of these ways of reacting must be dealt with as important elements in the situation—as important as the facts of the problem itself.

The social worker will need to bring to any situation not only understanding of its factual aspects, and knowledge of the available resources for dealing with them, but also sensitive understanding of the feelings of the people enmeshed in the problem; only thus can there be real ability to deal with them in ways that build up the clients' inner resources and capacity for self-help.

In light of this, what is it about the way in which all trained workers will approach their tasks that identifies what they do as a *professional* service?

There have been many attempts to define the term "profession"; there is now rather general agreement on its essential elements.

One of the most important of these is that a profession serves social rather than personal ends; that is, it is concerned with service of mankind rather than with private gain. In social work, commitment to this principle is expressed, in part, by members of the profession in common ways of thinking about the individual human being—his place and essential rights in the society of which he is a part—and about society's responsibility to him.

Social workers put it this way: "Social work as a profession is committed to the democratic ideal of equality of opportunity for all. True equality of opportunity implies freeing the individual, in so far as possible, from all the obstacles that stand in the way of his continued growth, whether these obstacles exist within himself, in his relationship to others, or in community conditions or attitudes. It is the ultimate goal of social work to help in the creation of this kind of personal freedom." *

It is when considering this aspect of the profession that social workers find themselves saying something like this:

I profess:

A profound belief in the worth of every human being, respect for his dignity, and commitment, in whatever I do, to protect his essential rights and freedoms;

An acceptance of people without regard to race, color, creed, or social or economic status, believing that this carries with it acceptance of the right of people to be different;

An acceptance of people as they are and a willingness to begin working with them where and as they are;

A commitment to a professional and creative use of relationships with people seeking help as the central means of giving aid, entering into such relationships not only with respect for the individual or individuals involved, but with belief in their innate capacity to share and contribute to the solution of the problem on which we are at work together;

* From the pamphlet *Social Work as a Profession*, issued by the Council on Social Work Education, 345 East 46th Street, New York 17, N.Y.

A belief that the participation of those we are seeking to help is essential for their self-respect and sense of accomplishment and that, while recognizing that people will differ in the degree of capacity and readiness to help themselves, there must always be honest sharing, free from manipulation in any form;

A determination to observe scrupulously the principle of confidentiality in dealing with the private concerns of people ʰat may be divulged in conference or in other contacts, belie, ʰg that regard for the worth and dignity of the individu... annot be served otherwise;

A respect for the right of the individual to his own point of view, even if it is at variance with mine;

A commitment never to superimpose my personal attitudes and standards of behavior, while simultaneously accepting a role as a representative of society with a duty to help those with whom I am working to assume responsibility—not only for themselves, but toward society itself—to obey the law, and to conform to society's accepted codes of behavior;

A fundamental acceptance of the right of people to run their own lives and make their own decisions, to reject as well as to accept help.

These are foundation beliefs that give direction to the way the social worker will act, whatever the situation calling for his particular skills; it is out of the stuff of these principles and values that a Code of Ethics * has been drawn up by the National Association of Social Workers for conscious and constant reference by the social worker in any and all of his activities.

Social work makes no claim to having a "corner" on these values. Many of them are part of our common heritage as Americans; other professions invoke them, and social-minded, humane, and non-self-seeking people everywhere subscribe to the truths they carry.

Social work as a profession can be fully understood, however, only as its services are seen as having a direct and constant relation to these values and as aiming, in undeviating

* See Appendix.

fashion, at the full realization of their promise for all people.

In its unequivocal dedication to all that will constitute a forward thrust toward social reform and in its staunch adherence to the values set down here, social work and social workers will inevitably find themselves in the midst of conflicts in attitudes and ways of thinking in American communities today. There will be people whose strong self-interest or lack of readiness for the full demands of a truly democratic way of life will challenge the values and beliefs held by the social worker. Human considerations get lost in a highly competitive society, and social work's concern for "where the chips may fall" will meet with limited response in some groups.

The social worker has to learn to meet these conflicting attitudes with poise and intelligence and with ever-increasing ability to demonstrate and interpret, without recrimination, what it is that his profession holds to be most important.

Another hallmark of a profession is that its members possess special competence in the performance of a service—a specialized and skillful way of doing things that is not possessed by everyone; this requirement is important for the safeguarding of those seeking service and for the protection of society itself. It serves, too, to establish a standard of competence, recognized and accepted by the profession as a whole, as a means of identifying and protecting its qualified members.

In some professions, professional competence is publicly proclaimed through a required process of certification, registration, or licensing by a public authority—an arm of the government. Except in California, which requires the registration of social workers, there is no overall public licensing requirement covering social workers. There is, however, a process of certification maintained by the National Association of Social Workers. With the establishment of an Academy of Certified Social Workers, the Association issues certificates to its members for specified periods of time during which qualifications are met.

Responsibility for setting the standards of competence in a particular field of service rests with the profession itself. In the early days of all professions, skills gained through doing were passed on to succeeding streams of new workers through apprenticeship plans. Leading practitioners of the professions, responsible for teaching in this way, began to reach out for insights and theoretical knowledge that would give deeper meaning to and greater accomplishments in their fields of practice. As a first step toward strengthening their practice and their teaching of practice, they began to establish special schools.

Later, these schools tended to move into universities as it became clear that their essential bodies of knowledge and skill rested upon basic sciences. Theory and practice were thus brought into close relationship, and the integration of these two kinds of knowledge remains a constant activity in specialized education for any profession. Recognition of the dependence of specialized practice on basic sciences led, too, to the conviction that a sound liberal education should precede professional preparation and to a view of the professional man or woman as "educated" in the broadest and deepest meaning of that term.

Social work, as a relatively young profession, has followed this same pattern of development, and today, as in other professions, its schools are integral parts of universities, where the preparation and accrediting of members of the profession are carried out in distinctly educational terms.

Standards of education to equip the social worker for professional-level performance are a primary concern of the Council on Social Work Education.* This organization "was established in July 1952, to 'promote sound programs of social work education in the United States and Canada.' Its constituency includes graduate professional schools of social work, undergraduate departments offering social welfare content introductory to professional social work, national agencies which employ social workers, the National Association of Social Workers and the interested public. Although the

* See Appendix.

Council serves as the recognized accrediting agency for graduate professional education, it has no accrediting function in undergraduate education. It does offer to undergraduate departments within its membership a variety of consultative and advisory services, publications and technical materials as well as opportunities for exchange of views and information." *

The Council publishes material addressed directly to those wishing to explore social work as a possible career. This includes a kit of instructive information about the profession, a list of the accredited graduate schools of social work in this country and Canada, and other useful publications.

The professional schools of social work, meeting the standards set by the accrediting bodies of the Council on Social Work Education, proclaim—through a process of academic graduation and presentation to the university of qualified candidates for a master's degree—that the graduating worker has mastered essential bodies of knowledge from his study in school classrooms and from fieldwork in a social agency and is now ready to give professional service to people.

As members of their profession, these graduating workers, in common with those already employed, will draw insights for their work from a common store of basic knowledge and, within their special areas of practice—case work, group work, or community organization—will observe principles and use methods that are recognizably the same from Maine to the Gulf and from California to the eastern seaboard.

An important point for emphasis in all of this is that education is at the heart of this profession, not only as a formal means of ensuring that its workers are competent, but as a dominant characteristic of the way in which they will serve people.

This means that professionally educated social workers are expected to apply to their work a free use of intelligence undergirded by substantial knowledge gained through intel-

* From the pamphlet *Social Welfare Content in Undergraduate Education*, issued by the Council on Social Work Education, 345 East 46th Street, New York 17, N.Y.

lectual effort. Drawing on all his sources of knowledge and understanding, the social worker must make a professional judgment as to what is involved in any given situation, determine how best to proceed in it, and decide what particular method or methods to use to deal with it. This means that not only *doing* but *thinking* is an essential element; this factor of independent judgment, drawing on intellectually acquired knowledge, differentiates the profession from other highly skilled occupations in which activity is routinized within narrowly set specifications. It should be understood, too, that this professional approach, calling for educated judgment, precludes moving into any situation on the basis of "hunch" or intuition.

One of the exciting things about all professions is their continuing expansion of relevant knowledge through the testing of experience and the findings of scientifically directed research. Research as a recognized means of increasing the body of knowledge on which the practitioner depends is an essential element in all professions; this reaching for more and more knowledge through study and scientifically disciplined research gives the professions, including social work, the right to be called "learned."

In Chapters Four and Five, the areas of knowledge considered essential both for basic undergraduate preparation in social work and for the curriculum of the professional school itself will be considered.

The role played by practitioners themselves in establishing a profession suggests that they will exert a strong influence on its continuing development and on the protection of its established standards of performance. This is the more true when, following a tendency of all professions, its practitioners draw together into a formal association for the promotion of their common interests and the advancement of the profession of which they are members.

In social work, this association of members is the National Association of Social Workers.* Working through commis-

* See Appendix.

sions and committees of members, the Association is constantly endeavoring to keep its members abreast of developments in the broad field of social welfare and to direct disciplined scrutiny of particular areas of practice methods. Members also function in local chapters from which representatives are elected as delegates to annual policy-making assemblies of the Association.

In addition to descriptive pamphlets and printed reports of particular pieces of exploration, the Association publishes a professional journal, *Social Work*, issued four times a year; this journal is described as "committed to improving practice and extending knowledge in the field of social welfare." Its editorial board invites "manuscripts that yield new insights into established practices, evaluate new techniques and research, examine current social problems, or bring serious critical analysis to bear on the problems of the profession itself."

This inner urge toward gaining more and more knowledge as a basis for increasing competence is of the essence in a profession. It grows out of a deep commitment not only to serve people but, in light of their innate worth, to serve them well. José Ortega y Gasset says, in *Toward a Philosophy of History*, "I cannot conceive of life without a vocation, an inner summons. The vocation arises from the vital spring, and from the vocation is born the project of life, which, at every moment, constitutes 'my life.' " *

By the nature of its services, social work makes special demands on the personality of its workers. Out of deep feelings of compassion for human beings, strong motivation to serve them, and willingness to undergo the disciplines of the required training, the learning worker discovers a new ideal of self—a closely meshed personal-professional self—for whom the chosen career becomes his "project of life" and, in a vital way, his "life" itself. This sense of vocation is at the heart of social work as a profession.

* José Ortega y Gasset, *Toward a Philosophy of History*, W. W. Norton & Company, Inc., New York, 1941.

4

How to Get Ready in College

While busy with your final years at college, you may also be raising questions about social work as a possible career; you may be wondering whether this profession would be a vital one for you and whether your personal qualities and academic qualifications will meet its requirements. If this is so, there are quite definite things you can do to get some of your questions at least partially answered.

Talk to People Who Know

Many such people are in your immediate vicinity. School guidance counselors, faculty advisers, and staff members of local social agencies can be turned to for information. An officer or member of a local chapter of the National Association of Social Workers or a faculty member in a nearby school of social work could give you valuable help.

Outstanding social workers in active practice or serving on the faculty of a graduate school of social work may visit your campus to participate in a careers-day program; if time is allowed for individual interviews after the program, this would be a good follow-up occasion.

You may already be doing volunteer work in a local social agency, either as part of a student social service project or in connection with one of your courses. Making an opportunity

32

to talk with professional social workers on the agency's staff will usually be well worth the trouble.

You yourself or a member of your family may have occasion to use the help of a social agency, with a resulting opportunity for close and direct contact with a practicing social worker.

Perhaps in your home community or during vacation time you will have the best opportunity for direct contact. Members of your family may already know social workers through the volunteer service they themselves are giving on boards and committees or in direct work with patients in a hospital or with participants in a settlement house or community center.

A little beforehand thinking on your part will help clarify the questions you want to ask and will make it easier for the people you approach to be really helpful to you.

Test Your Interests and Abilities

Getting information is only the first step. Most students can find further ways to explore the requirements for social work. You probably participate in certain campus activities; perhaps you have a particular responsibility in the YMCA, YWCA, or Hillel, in the student government council or a special-interest club. There are many opportunities in such assignments for you to check on how well you get along with other people—an aptitude of supreme importance for social work.

A chance to try yourself out in a direct program of helping people holds real possibilities. If you are not already doing some form of volunteer service that makes this possible, it might be a good idea to seek this kind of experience. Your department director, an interested professor, or a student adviser would probably be glad to explore the possibility with you and help you figure out a way of doing actual work without neglecting your courses.

In some of the larger cities,* social work recruiting com-

* See Appendix for list.

mittees have worked out careful plans for helping students get summer jobs in a variety of health and welfare agencies. Students who qualify for this experience are referred directly to the agencies. Jobs are salaried and last approximately eight weeks. The specific job may be as a case aide in a family or children's agency or in the medical social service department of a hospital or an agency for social services in a psychiatric institution; it may be as an assistant group worker or counselor in a day or resident camp sponsored by a settlement house or a community center.

The job may involve home visits with a social worker or helping a hospitalized patient to obtain a needed appliance or participating in the referral of clients to other agencies for special services. It may mean helping children in a community center to work off their boundless energies in constructive group activities—and working through the children to reach their families. Employment as counselor in a resident summer camp provides the opportunity for close and continuous contact with children, for gaining insight on many aspects of human behavior, and for getting a clearer view of those problems and needs that call for social welfare services.

An especially helpful feature of this summer experience plan is that you receive direct supervision from a trained social worker who has been designated as the person to help you know the agency, become acquainted with the community in which it operates, and increase your understanding of the problems and unmet needs of the people the agency is organized to serve.

The supervisor will be the direct source of help on the doing of the particular job; in weekly conferences, there will be time to explore the meaning of things that happen day by day on the job, and you will get advice about how to get to know the people that the job touches—the "whys" of what you meet and see and the "hows" of carrying out your particular part of the agency's program of service. In dealing directly with matters related to the job itself, there will be opportunity to talk with one who knows and understands your feelings of both satisfaction and frustration. Since this is preeminently a time for self-testing, questions about depth of interest and whether interest grows or lessens are legitimate business in the conferences with the supervisor.

There are usually opportunities, too, in these summer programs, for the student workers to get together in group sessions to discuss major social problems, social welfare programs related to these problems, social work as a profession, and the role of social workers in giving service and in working for social change.

A summer job in a social welfare agency, volunteer service in an agency in the college community, and a beginning job after college are all useful occasions for the kind of self-testing that should precede an individual decision about social work as a professional career. This is because they provide an opportunity for a careful weighing of aptitudes, abilities, qualities, skills, and experience in direct relation to the doing of a specific job; actual work experience contributes immeasurably to understanding of what the profession desires and expects.

You will bring two things to any job—now or in the future: your innate qualities and capacities and your acquired knowledge and learned skills. Later in this chapter there will be a consideration of the basic knowledge to be acquired in college that will provide the educational foundation on which a subsequent program of professional education for social work can be built. Meanwhile, there are some trustworthy guides as to what are considered essential qualities and qualifications for professional practice in social work. Against these you should consider and test out your own personal qualities, your attitudes, what you regard as very important in life, your emerging goals for the future, and your education, experience, and proven abilities up to this point.

Assess Your Qualifications

In any thoughtful consideration of social work, it becomes crystal clear that it has to do centrally and all the time with people. How we think about people is crucial. Applicants for admission to a school of social work often say, "I like people," or, "I want to work with people." This, however, may not be enough unless it is accompanied by evidence of deep and genuine concern for them and willingness to undergo the disciplines of learning how to work with them sensitively, knowledgeably, and in a professional manner.

Working with people as a social worker means, of course, working with all kinds of people. There can be no fencing in, for our helping efforts, of those people who appeal to us personally—people we like—while others remain outside in a sort of no-man's-land. What has seemed a strong desire to work with people has sometimes crumbled a bit with the realization that "people" will include the unlovely, the selfish, the manipulative—even the cruel—as well as the friendly, the unselfish, the generous, and the cooperative.

This suggests careful thinking about how you customarily react to people who seem very different from yourself and careful scrutiny of any lurking prejudices.

In the professional school, there will be concentrated study of why people behave as they do; this professional approach, based on a nonjudgmental and objective way of thinking about and acting toward people and their problems has been said to "combine understanding based on knowledge, with acceptance based on faith in the worth of every human being." This cannot be acquired by persons who have deeply rooted prejudices which they are in no mood to change or who withdraw from behavior which, in personal terms, they find distasteful.

A sense of humor will help the social worker over some hurdles in the day's work and will give scope to a needed light touch; it goes without saying that a real sense of humor does not express itself in caustic or hurtful barb and that, generally speaking, it is directed toward situations and not persons.

It will be important, too, to get a view of yourself in continuous relationships with people; your relations with family and friends should be included in your thinking. The art of relating constructively to others, whether they be clients, coworkers, board members, or the janitor, is of central importance in social work. Ability in the thoughtful and sensitive use of all relationships is a matter of considered growth in the professional school, but experience tells us that its growth has little chance if a capacity for relating to people has not already been developed in the student's earlier life experience. Learning to work warmly and helpfully with people would come very hard for the person who had been deprived of satisfactory relationships as he grew up.

How the person considering social work has come to terms with all the elements in his own life experience—its lights and shadows, accomplishments and failures, opportunities and limitations—is of deep significance. Complete solution or adjustment may not yet have been reached, but carrying into social work a high degree of preoccupation with one's own concerns or personal difficulties leaves little room or energy for becoming mindful of and active toward the concerns and problems of others.

The professional schools are looking for better-than-average, not "just-getting-by," intellectual ability. Personality qualities are recognizedly important for social work, but they cannot take the place of mental curiosity, capacity for thinking clearly, and ability to assemble pertinent facts for use as a base for action. In social work, thinking is as important as doing, and the prospective social worker needs to face the fact that graduate study will demand a high level of intellectual effort.

Assessment of an applicant's intellectual capacity is accompanied by consideration of the breadth of his social awareness, and evidence of intelligent interest in broad social issues is looked for. The college campus is rare that is without opportunities for its students to think about and involve themselves in areas of major social concern. The hope would be that the student applicant had taken full advantage of such opportunities and had developed both interest and facility in discussions of the concerns he has learned about.

Of particular importance for anyone looking toward a social work career is awareness of the major social and economic ills and of the alignments and interrelations of business, industry, political movements, and government.

What is going on in the rest of the world and how that affects our domestic affairs and the development of our own international policy should be an area of concern. It will serve you well, too, to be increasingly well informed about the patterns of life emerging in our country—its interracial and intercultural relationships, what is happening at the core of our great cities, and developments in the relations of city and suburbia and town and country. Eyes and ears alerted to capture from the pages of the public press, from articles in the magazines, from commentary on radio and TV, and from utterances of the country's leaders the current trends in thinking about the affairs of men and nations will stimulate and broaden your own understanding of these essential matters.

The lives of ordinary people are caught up, day by day, in these larger issues; to understand them is to develop ever-deeper conviction about the need to place human values above all other considerations and to recognize that the social worker's irrevocable stance is one that is against whatever creates injustice or denies equality of opportunity for all people.

Plan Your College Program

The gathering of information, the pursuit of self-testing opportunities in a social agency, and the careful assessment of personal qualities and qualifications should be accompanied by a thoughtful approach to what, in light of an interest in social work, should appropriately enter into your undergraduate program of study.

A baccalaureate degree in arts, letters, philosophy, or science from an accredited college or university is a basic requirement for entering a professional school of social work.

The question remains as to what course content in college will contribute most effectively to your acquiring a sound educational base on which to build and make the best use of a later program of professional education at the graduate level.

As a matter of fact, nothing in the customary curriculum of a good liberal arts college is patently "off-side" for a career in social work. Professional schools do not, in rigid fashion, specify particular courses as prerequisites for admission. They establish their own selective base and admit students presenting varieties of undergraduate education. It is recognized, however, that a program drawn from a broad range of courses in the humanities and social and biological sciences * can contribute usefully to preparation for entrance into such schools. Several schools, in connection with their expectation of the completion of sixty semester hours in the liberal arts, specify the inclusion of a minimum of twenty semester hours in the social and biological sciences.

Inevitably you will have some choice of courses, and this should not be an "at-random" affair! There are important matters to think about in consultation with your school adviser or department director. The best results will probably flow from such a joint bit of exploration when you have brought together:

1. Examination of characteristic professional school statements concerning educational requirements for admission. (Catalogs are available.)
2. A careful look at the offerings in your own school.
3. Consideration of your own intellectual interests and areas of particular social concern, with regard for your own individual flair.

UNDERSTANDING PEOPLE

Because social work as a profession is primarily concerned with people and their social functioning, undergraduate course content must provide a core of essential knowledge of man

---

* The humanities are generally considered to include languages, literature, philosophy, religion, the classics, and art; social sciences include anthropology, economics, history, political science, psychology, and sociology; biological sciences are botany, biology, physiology, zoology, and the like. (*Note:* Many psychologists prefer listing with the biological sciences.)

himself and of what enters into all aspects of human growth and behavior—physical, intellectual, emotional, cultural, spiritual, and social. It would be well if, along with study of the ways in which different sciences analyze and explain the behavior of people as they react to others and to circumstances in their life experience, there was an opportunity for considering some of the patterns of group association and the ways of behaving that groups develop. Of particular importance for a future social worker would be early learning about the family, peer groups in childhood, and work and professional groups in adult life, with consideration of their influence on the development of their members. The understanding of the individual and the group learned in this way will provide the necessary foundation for professional social work courses on the dynamics of human growth and behavior, psychosocial pathology, and group and social processes.

Man's Environment—Sociocultural, Political, and Economic

We Americans live in cities and towns and villages. Since the field of social welfare is primarily concerned with man interacting in society, substantial material from the social sciences will be relevant for potential social workers. Particularly significant knowledge includes concepts of social organization and disorganization, social structures and systems, social role and status, and social change, conflict, and control. Courses that contain material on the family and the community, on problems of industrialization, urbanization, population growth, and mobility would be very good.

Because of the great diversity of people applying for social services, it is important to master basic knowledge about cultural difference from courses considering ethnic groups, culture conflicts, problems of social adjustment, and the ways in which maladjustment shows itself. There should be attention, too, to the relation of cultural background to social role and to the development of individual personality.

The curriculum of the professional school will include an

emphasis on sociocultural elements in social work practice; for your fieldwork there, you would very likely be placed in an agency serving people of markedly different cultural background, and the securing of basic knowledge in this area while still in college would serve you well.

As we continue to think of people and their multiple relationships in any community, we see that the government— national, state, county, or municipality—will enter their lives at many points. Children must go to school for specified periods of time; if they leave school early, they must receive a government permit to go to work. There are formal provisions to cover an infinite variety of contractual relationships and the ways in which an individual will conduct himself in relation to other people and to public and private property. Forces of law and order see to the observance of these provisions, and their violation can bring arrest and punishment under the law. These relations with the government mean, further, that one family's budget will include the payment of taxes to maintain these and many other phases of government services, while another family, because of dire need, may currently be the recipients of public assistance or other financial benefits under the government insurance schemes.

The social worker, in close relation to the day-by-day living problems of his clients, will inevitably be in contact with these and other aspects of government authority. Learning in professional school to work intelligently and helpfully in these relationships will be faster for the student who, from college courses with political science content, already has a good grasp of the philosophy, structure, and function of government at its various levels, its lines of authority, how public policy is formed, and how citizen action can influence change in policy.

Study of the basic elements in constitutional, statutory, and common law, the processes of public taxation and public administration, and the phenomenon of bureaucracy would also provide knowledge particularly important for the social worker.

The individual in his community—the heart of our interest and concern—will, to a greater or lesser degree, be in touch with a variety of nongovernmental institutions that will strongly influence his mode of living and his attitudes. Some of these will be closely connected with the economic developments of his community. If he is at work, he may be a member of a union or of an employers' association; in any case, his interests and well-being will be affected strongly by fluctuations in the economic system within which he lives.

Many of the human problems with which the social worker deals have their basis in economics. In professional school, there will be opportunity to study methods of working intelligently with those whose family life has been disrupted because of the unemployment of its breadwinner; because of lack of access to jobs, owing to inadequacy of preparation for today's technical demands; because of school dropouts who are unable to find jobs; or because of low wage standards and poor working conditions and hardships growing out of labor conflicts and extended periods of strike. The professional social work student will deal more readily with situations in which these elements are paramount if he brings from college courses sound knowledge about economic enterprise and development in modern society, economic welfare theory, and the intimate interrelationships of income, prices, wages, and standards of living. Obviously there should be knowledge, too, of the place and role of labor in America, of government-industry and labor-management relations, of current forms of labor organization, and of methods of collective bargaining.

Being a social worker means working in a real community, within the realities and pressures of *its* conditions of life, to help people deal constructively with their problems in living; many of these problems grow out of the very community conditions suggested for study in your college courses.

In professional school, the student will learn to deal directly with maladjustments and sufferings related to these conditions; and that learning will advance more surely if it is built on a solid foundation of knowledge drawn from a college curriculum that has included course content dealing specifically with the sociocultural, political, and economic environment within which people live.

BUT PEOPLE CAN NEVER BE FULLY UNDERSTOOD ON THE BASIS SOLELY OF THE "HERE AND NOW"

People come "trailing clouds of glory"—and of tragedy—from the past. The wide reaches of history that stretch out behind them are filled with the richness and the poignancy of human experience. Study that does not include some reaching back into man's cultural heritage cannot be expected to give understanding of the values by which he lives today—what has meaning for him, his aspirations, urgencies, and feelings of incompleteness, and the sources to which he looks for fulfillment and satisfaction of some of his deepest desires.

Social welfare institutions are themselves man-made, and the values of successive groups of dedicated men and women have gone into their development and support. Understanding of the motives that brought services into being will light up later and more concentrated study in professional school of the origins of social welfare programs.

Social work itself rests a claim to professional status, in part, on a system of values related to the inherent worth and dignity of man—values that give direction to every aspect of service in which its workers are engaged. Sensitivity to human aspirations, values, and standards of behavior will be deepened through course content drawn from history, philosophy, and religion. A major contribution of philosophy and religion lies in the insights into human conduct that come from familiarity with man's cultural heritage.

It may be that in the study of one or more of the aesthetic and lively arts there will come further discoveries about people and their deepest yearnings. The gamut of human experience can be traced through the imagery of poetry, fine fiction, and drama; it finds expression in the surge of music, in the movement of the dance, in sculptural form, and on the living canvases of the great artists.

Scientific Thinking and Precise Analysis

Social work and social workers are primarily concerned with problem-solving. Every day they are dealing with problems in the relations of people—problems arising from deprivation, from unemployment or impaired health; problems inherent in the experience of living in inadequate homes, in surroundings of squalor and crime, often in a climate of dissension and intergroup conflict—experiences, all of them, that give the lie to the promise of equal opportunity for all.

Ability to deal expertly with such problems does not come by any magic route or by the waving of a wand in the professional school; it comes the hard way, through patient and disciplined handling of essential steps in the problem-solving process. What in the content of the college curriculum can help create the mood for such a scientific approach and afford some experience in its use? Courses that give particular emphasis to the importance of orderly and systematic arrangement of facts and ideas and to the formulation of working hypotheses as an approach to problem-solving will make a contribution here.

Some development of this ability could be looked for in dealing with problems and propositions in mathematics, in exercises in a logic course, or possibly in some direct experience with beginning research methods in a variety of courses. Whatever the opportunity for practice, it should foster a serious mood of inquiry, respect for facts, willingness to go where they take you, and commitment to the necessary disciplines of scientific method in putting tested findings to work. The student endowed with a lively mental curiosity can find support and deep satisfaction as the disciplines acquired in this way give significant answers to questions and uncover hitherto unrealized insights for understanding.

The Spoken and the Written Word

Social workers, constantly working with people, are under the sharp necessity of developing more and more skill at putting ideas into meaningful and easily communicable forms. Appropriate choice of the word to be spoken or the phrase to be used and ease and comfortableness with language are vital in relating directly and helpfully to a wide range of people. Social workers write letters, too, and are held responsible for accurate recording of their activities; they prepare reports for groups inside and outside the agency. Ability to express ideas clearly and with respect both for content and for those who must hear, read, and understand is essential.

The professional school looks to the college to instill in its students an appreciation for this necessity of clear communication in all relationships and expects its courses to provide opportunity for direct exercise. "Too late" may be the professional school's admissions judgment of the candidate whose application materials and correspondence indicate that he has not mastered basic skills in this area or achieved respect for the use he will make of them.

Courses in English, wide reading with attention to style as well as content, college debating society or discussion forum experience, together with faculty requirements for lucidity in papers and oral presentations, should be regarded as opportunities for development in this really important area of communication.

What has been suggested up to this point is summed up by the Council on Social Work Education: "In all colleges and universities courses are available, in the first and second years, which would communicate a beginning understanding of man and society, an introduction to the methods of problem-solving and the arts of communication, and an awareness of historical movements and philosophical thought." *

Customarily it is in the third and fourth years that students concentrate in a specified area or areas of study. It is in this period that, along with advanced content in basic disciplines,

* From the pamphlet *Social Welfare Content in Undergraduate Education*, issued by the Council on Social Work Education, 345 East 46th Street, New York 17, N.Y.

your school may offer introductory courses on the profession itself.

COURSES IN SOCIAL WELFARE AND SOCIAL WORK

The value of such course content is obvious. Where it is included, the hope of the professional school would be that it is built on solid educational foundations in the areas already mentioned and not developed as something apart.

From such courses, students should gain an appreciation of social welfare as an expression of society's concern for people and their well-being. There should be information on the origins and types of problems that social welfare programs are organized to meet and an opportunity to gain understanding of how, through the years, society has moved to prevent and remedy social ills.

Since social welfare is involved in the processes of government at all levels, the student should be expected to gain an understanding of political pressures, the formation of public opinion, the force of political action in influencing public policy, and the legislative changes directly affecting social welfare programs.

Economic theory takes a large place in the study of social welfare. Consideration of what makes for economic security will help in the understanding of existing social insurance programs—how they came to be and what their influence has been on living standards.

One of the major goals of courses on social work as a profession should be to introduce the student to the several roles of the social worker, the values and activities of social work, and the settings in which it is practiced. The profession needs to be understood within the context of the country's total program of social welfare and within the framework of all helping professions. Previously gained knowledge of social roles will be useful in examining the professional role of the social worker within a social agency and as a member of a profession.

An opportunity to see this profession in its relation to other helping professions and educational disciplines should answer questions you may have had as to what constitutes the difference between psychiatry and psychology on the one hand and social work on the other. It should make clear that psychiatry, as a branch of the medical profession, is concerned with the diagnosis, treatment, and prevention of mental illness and that psychology's contribution is through research, personality testing, and clinical exploration. Social workers, however, although they often work in a close team relationship with psychiatrists and psychologists, should be seen as working first, and all the time, to develop or restore the social functioning of individuals, families, groups, and communities.

There may have been confusion, too, about sociology and social work. A college course on social work should help clarify that sociology, as a science and an area of knowledge, will be drawn on heavily by social workers. The skills of the social worker using this knowledge will be directed, however, to dealing directly with social problems, in efforts to help real people meet and solve them. Graduate study in sociology alone does not prepare a person for professional practice in social work.

There should be a beginning clarification of this profession's approach to the solving of problems and, particularly, how this approach enters into its three major practice methods —case work, group work, and community organization. A course providing descriptive material on all of these methods is sounder that a one-sided concentration on any one.

Further materials should familiarize the student with the major social agencies that primarily serve people individually or as a part of a family unit and with the characteristic role of their case workers as working with people in trouble on a one-by-one basis. Other social agencies should be seen as placing primary emphasis on working with people in groups.

Because confusion sometimes arises over the difference between recreation work, on the one hand, and group work as a method in social work, on the other, the course should help the student see their differences. Recreation is a broad field using many methods; it gives continuing emphasis to the enjoyment per se of a chosen activity and provides for the learning of specific recreational skills as a means of enjoyment for its own sake. The provision of recreational activities is characteristic of most communities today, under both commercial and private and public auspices.

Group work, as one of the three recognized methods in social work, seeks to provide values beyond the learning of a recreational skill and enjoyment of an activity. The group worker uses the group experience itself and the interrelationships of group members as means of contributing to the growth and adjustment of individuals. He seeks to promote development of emotional stability and maturity; and by encouraging democratic ways of conducting the group's affairs, he assists the learning of social skills that can be turned to the service of society.

Community organization as a method of social work practice will undoubtedly be shown as concerned with planning and coordinating social welfare services on a neighborhood or total community basis. Its workers give professional leadership to citizen groups that assume responsibility for assuring services to meet the health and welfare needs of all the people in a community.

Clear descriptions of these roles in a course that predates or follows immediately upon a testing-out work experience in a social agency should give added color and meaning to that experience. At the same time, it should provide some trustworthy guidelines for determining—once a decision for a social work career is reached—which of the three practice methods to pursue in professional school. This decision may not be absolute before reaching professional school— and advisory help will be available there for further exploration—but it would be well to take every opportunity for acquaintance with these methods.

Obviously no one student will be able to acquire, in equal degree and depth, foundation knowledge in all the areas that have been suggested as relevant. This is why desirable content has been presented in rather broad terms and not as rigidly bounded within specifically titled courses. Courses in different departments and disciplines will conceivably contribute more than heavy concentration in one area. There will be an organizational question, particularly within the upper years of undergraduate education, as to how to group together courses from several departments to provide the essential body of knowledge suggested.

Most of the colleges and universities that now offer a planned program in the area of social welfare place responsibility for it in the sociology department. A significant amount of content is added from economics, political science, psychology, anthropology, and other disciplines that, in all probability, has not been completely covered in the first two years of general education. In colleges and universities that have established divisions of social science or social studies, much of the suggested content could be covered to a large extent in offerings in such a division.

Within the actualities of the curriculum offered in your school, the aim should be, through careful course selection and continuous cross-referencing of knowledge gained from many sources, to build as strong a foundation as possible on which to build a later program of professional education at the graduate level.

Considerations dealt with in this chapter should be held in close relation to what follows immediately, in Chapter Five, on the educational program of the professional school. Together, they form a continuous story of the making of a social worker who will be well equipped for the demands he or she will face and who, with graduation from the professional school, will be ready for practice in a profession that so sorely needs steadily increasing numbers of qualified men and women.

5

How to Get Ready
in Professional
School

Is Professional Education Necessary?

Perhaps, looking back over the years in college, the question arises as to whether there are not opportunities for jobs in the broad field of social welfare without two further years in a professional school and a graduate degree in social work. The answer is: Yes, there are.

This is a field of acute personnel shortage, and there are not enough trained people to meet its rapidly expanding demands. Many agencies have employed untrained people to carry out some aspects of their services; few of these agencies, however, regard the in-service training programs they have had to institute as valid substitutes for professional education. As vacancies occur and as new and excitingly challenging opportunities for service develop, agencies are moving, at noticeably faster speed, to step up their personnel requirements; their preference for workers with professional education is clearly stated in their published vacancy descriptions.

In individual terms, then, the comparison begins to narrow down to the difference between a professional career in the field and employment with a limited and, in many instances, a precarious future.

Over and over again, highly motivated workers, with unquestioned ideals for quality of service but without professional education to support them, have expressed deep feelings of disquietude over their lack of preparedness for their work and the frustration that comes in jobs inevitably hemmed in by inadequacies in knowledge and insight and by inability to act with the sureness of trained and disciplined workers.

Deep concern for people and a desire to help are essential qualities for all entering social work, but more is needed than caring and a will to help. As in all professions, preparation for social work calls for a program of specialized education; there are no short cuts.

Two years of full-time study for a master's degree in a graduate professional school is the established requirement for anyone desiring to qualify as a professional social worker.

The Professional Schools

There are sixty-four accredited schools of social work in the United States and Canada,* all of them attached to universities. To be accredited, a school must meet and continue to meet standards established by the Council on Social Work Education. While standards are uniform, not all the schools offer opportunity for concentrated study in all three of the methods of social work.

Several of the schools, in addition to their two-year program leading to a master's degree, provide for advanced study beyond that point, in programs leading either to a third-year certificate or to a doctor of science degree.

Filing an Application

Personal considerations—possibly direct acquaintanceship with a university and its school—as well as the size of the school, its geographic location, the type of community in which it operates, and the precise nature of its program or its

* Listed in the Appendix.

tuition costs may enter into the selection of a school or
schools to which to apply.

All the schools maintain admissions offices; a letter of inquiry will set in motion a school's selective admission process in relation to you. Early application is advisable. Precise
information about the time is usually included in a school's
catalog and should be noted.

When the school receives a request to consider a candidate,
its response is accompanied by rather comprehensive application materials; the forms differ from school to school, but
they are generally alike in what they ask for. This includes
basic social data, as well as factual information, in transcript
form, on formal education at the undergraduate level. As
stated earlier, the educational requirement for admission to a
graduate professional school is a bachelor's degree in arts or
science from a college approved by the university to which
application is being made.

The school will also inquire about any preprofessional work
experience, on either a volunteer or a paid basis, and there
will be a request for the names of persons who, knowing the
candidate well as an individual, will be able to comment on
his essential qualities and his proven abilities in school and
in jobs. There will be questions about health and also about
plans for financing a two-year educational program.

Most of the schools will ask the candidate to submit a
freely written account describing the development of his interest in social work and giving his own view of his motivation and qualifications for this profession. He will probably
be asked to make some reference to things in his life experience that have influenced his career decision.

All the schools require, where it is humanly possible, that
the candidate be interviewed by a qualified person, usually
an alumnus. When no qualified alumnus is geographically
available, the candidate is referred to a member of a national
roster of interviewers maintained by the Council on Social
Work Education; the interviewer's report in such a situation
can be made available to more than one school if the candidate wishes.

The purpose of the interview is to provide a face-to-face opportunity for joint exploration of the candidate's qualifications for entering a school of social work; it should give him firsthand information about the school and its educational program and supplement his growing awareness of the demands of social work as a profession. Free discussion of his interests and life experience will help the candidate and his interviewer to explore together how his qualifications meet requirements for undertaking graduate professional study in this field. The interviewer does not make the admissions decision; he submits his report to the school admissions office, where it becomes one part of the accumulating material.

When all the materials requested have been received, they are assembled into an inclusive individual folder for careful reading. In this reading, the materials are dealt with in their entirety—each part in relation to all the others. No one element stands alone as the determining factor in selection; the effort is, rather, to get a composite picture of the candidate's qualifications.

In short, the aim of the admissions procedure is to help the candidate and the school determine whether the essential personal and intellectual qualifications are present and whether the candidate is equipped to undergo the disciplines and is ready to meet the demands of a program of graduate professional education.

The Cost of Professional Education

All professional education is costly, not only in the time it takes but in the financial outlay it represents. Social work is no exception. The actual money cost to complete two years of graduate education will vary somewhat with the school selected, of course, and with the candidate's living situation—whether he will be living on his own or with his family.

Generally speaking, tuition costs are lowest in the tax-supported state or municipal universities; costs are higher in the schools affiliated with privately endowed universities. This means that expenditures for tuition will range between free

tuition and fees of from $1,200 to $1,400 a year. Tuition
costs do not, however, constitute the largest part of the expense involved. A major item will be the total living cost.
This expense, too, will vary, depending on the price levels
in the particular community and the kind of living facilities
it offers. A student not living at home might need approximately $2,500 a year, paralleling, on the average, the annual
expenditure for living during the period of undergraduate
education.

While the financial problem may loom large at the outset,
it will be well to carry into every aspect of its consideration
the assurance that this cost is a capital investment in the
future. No other route can be expected to lead to comparable
returns in terms of expanding career opportunities, self-real-
ization and accomplishment, satisfactions on the job and a
good level of financial security; these prospects should be
given full weighting when the need to interrupt or defer
money earnings presses hard.

Financial Assistance

If the cost of professional education is beyond the candidate's immediate financial resources, he will want to consider
the availability of financial assistance. There are a substantial
number of fellowships, scholarships, noninterest loans, and
work-study grants in varying amounts that should be ex-
plored.

The school selected may have such funds available to cover
tuition in total or in part or to provide for some of the living
expense. Several national, state, and local agencies—both governmental and private—and a number of foundations also
offer stipends to cover all or part of the expense involved.
Competition for all types of student financial aid is keen, and
an applicant will need to be alert to the requirements, specific
provisions, and expectations in a given situation. Generally
speaking, grants are awarded on the basis of professional
promise and financial need. A list of sources of aid and the

kind of help they offer can be secured from the National Commission for Social Work Careers.*

Whatever the nature of financial need, it should enter into a candidate's early approach to a school; it constitutes a very important part of the "to-and-from" correspondence.

In all this financial planning, it is wise to keep in mind a statement from the pamphlet *Social Work as a Profession*. Speaking of many avenues leading to the goal of a master's degree in social work, it says simply: "Professional education may be postponed, but should not be by-passed if you are interested in a professional career as a social worker."

If it is impossible to finance two years of graduate school immediately after finishing college, perhaps you can plan a "by-stages" approach in which you attend school for one year and then take a beginning job in a social agency of good standards until a scholarship is available or you have saved enough for the second year. If such a plan is impossible, a beginning job might be secured immediately after graduation from college and serve similarly as a stepping-stone.

Local public welfare departments, councils of social agencies, or branches of national private agencies will have information on the availability of such job opportunities.**

In the interest of sound preparation for a full program of professional study, an important consideration in a preprofessional education job would be the quality of supervision provided; it would be well, in applying, to inquire about this; supervision by a qualified, professionally educated social worker can make the job a valuable learning experience. Your own approach to such an interim job is important too; to regard it as merely a "marking-time" episode might well hamper your best use of it and possibly lessen its value as experience to carry with you back to school.

The question is sometimes raised whether it is possible to combine professional education with a full-time job. If you are working in a community where there **is a** professional

* See Appendix.
** Partial list in Appendix.

school of social work, you may be able to take a limited
number of courses available for part-time students. Generally
speaking, taking such courses does not ensure admission to
full-time study, and there would be some limit to the number
of credits earned in this way that you could apply later to
a full-time program.

With very few exceptions, the program for the master of
science degree calls for four terms of full-time study, or approximately two years.

In some of the work-study plans instituted by certain
schools, in cooperation with selected social agencies, a student
receiving a study stipend from the agency in which he is
placed for field instruction will devote to that agency's program a very limited number of hours beyond those designated
for his fieldwork. He is considered a full-time student in the
school.

The Curriculum

It can be said of social work, as of all the helping professions, that in the nature of its educational preparation and
in its ways of putting its prescribed areas of knowledge to
work in serving people, it is both a science and an art.

The learning social worker is expected to acquire an ac-
cumulation of knowledge drawn from the arts and sciences
and from other professional disciplines, but in close association with this intellectual effort there is the necessity for
developing deepening disciplines and skill in the art of using
that knowledge in his day-to-day working relations with
people. It is not a case of pursuing knowledge for its own
sake, and knowledge alone is not enough. It will equip the
worker with insights that give him understanding of people
and their situations, of social forces and social structures,
and of social movements and trends in thinking; but the
professional man and woman is always faced with the necessity of learning, just as deeply, how to put his resources of
knowledge into active use in the service of human beings.

For the social work student, this means that, with continuous reference to his growing body of knowledge and with constant adherence to his profession's system of values, he must learn how to enter situations with people and use himself in ways that will enhance the essential dignity and maintain the self-esteem of those he seeks to serve, ensuring that their particular needs are being met with compassion and sensitive understanding. This calls for the learning of an art —an art with its own disciplines that have to be mastered and internalized until they become an essential part of the social worker himself, coloring everything he does.

The purpose of the professional schools, through their curriculum, is not only to impart the knowledge he needs, but to help the student with this knowledge to develop artistic skill in working creatively with people and to encourage his assumption of professional attitudes and disciplines. Taken together and closely interwoven, these elements make up the art and science of the profession.

The schools seek to accomplish this objective through a two-year closely integrated program of classroom and field instruction, library study and research, leading to a master's degree from the university of which they are a part. The emphasis in both classroom and field instruction is on what constitutes basic education for social work as a professional career, rather than on more narrowly conceived technical preparation for specific fields of social work activity in particular settings.

To amplify this approach a bit, before proceeding to deal with curriculum in more detail, it is believed that every social worker needs:

To know as much as he can possibly learn about the nature and dynamics of human relationships;

To understand the influence of environment on personal and social growth and development;

To learn to use himself and his knowledge with sensitive regard for the people he is seeking to help—their essential differences, their emotional and physical resources,

their aspirations and innate capacities, their needs, both
fancied and real, their reactions to other people and the
quality of their relationships with them;

To be alert to the potentialities for change and growth
both in the individual human being and in society itself;

To comprehend, through theoretical study, tested in real
situations, the strengths in the structures of society, as
well as the difficulties and problems they can impose on
people;

To be alert, knowledgeable, and ready to move responsi-
bly when opportunities emerge for influencing the direction of social change.

Courses designed by the schools to equip the learning social
worker in these areas of knowledge and skill will fall roughly
into three main categories.

SOCIAL WELFARE SERVICES

Building on undergraduate study in the social sciences,
which should have given foundation knowledge of social and
economic, cultural and political forces, the professional school
seeks to sharpen the focus on these elements. The student
gains a deeper appreciation of the social climate they have
produced in the nation as a whole and a quickened awareness
of the conditions they have created for the everyday living
of men, women, and children in its thousands of communities.

Seen against this background, the story of the development
of social services in this country becomes vivid, as changes
in social values, objectives, and methods of putting intentions
into operation are traced. There is continuous drawing on
knowledge from other fields—particularly law and economics—as services to meet the pressing needs of particular
groups in the population are studied. For example the urgency
for protective care of neglected, dependent, or delinquent
children will usually get special attention in the curriculum.

The relation of government to social welfare is a central
theme in this area of instruction, and the social worker emerging from two years in graduate school is expected to have

learned, with accuracy, what now constitute the social services provided through public departments of health and welfare, the courts, schools, and social insurance schemes. The system of social security by which loss of income is mitigated will come in for special study, and current problems of the high cost of medical care and the hardships arising from mental or physical disability will get concentrated attention.

From this whole area of study, students are expected to gain substantial knowledge of the major contemporary social services, both voluntary and governmental.

Another piece of the mosaic slips into place with study of the dynamic development of social work as a profession in this country. Various periods in its history are analyzed for understanding of its developing philosophy and for putting into bold relief, for the learning worker, the emerging roles of the social worker today as he assumes professional responsibility for furthering and strengthening the social services that give promise of a richer, more meaningful life for all Americans.

In his placement for field instruction in a social agency, the student gets a close look at the aims and characteristics of a particular program of social service and gains firsthand experience in giving service.

Human Growth and Behavior

To work creatively and helpfully with a human being, whatever his immediate problem or need, calls for as clear an understanding as possible of that person's ways of thinking and acting. It is not surprising, therefore, that careful instruction in human growth and behavior assumes central importance in the curriculum of a school of social work. Study in this area continues steadily, and in depth, throughout the two-year period.

The real people the student meets in the field instruction agency are immediately challenging in their infinite diversity, and it becomes very clear that no superficial approach will suffice. Two problems may, on the surface, look very much alike, but the ways of working through to a solution may differ in important ways because of the amazing differences presented by the persons involved. There will be differences in the way they see and feel about their problem, in the strengths they bring to its consideration, and in their reactions to the other people involved; differences in their hopes and fears, their reticences or readiness to share and participate. Because people are unique, to work with them creatively calls not only for sure knowledge to aid understanding but for disciplined artistry in its use.

Undergraduate study has given an opportunity to learn essential things about the nature of man; the professional school will build on this as it takes its students into further reaches of knowledge about growth and development in its normal aspects as well as into deeper understanding of all that indicates deviation from the normal.

Nothing quite equals the excitement and satisfaction that comes with learning to use this knowledge in working directly with people as skill develops in helping them find and respect their own inner capacities for dealing with their troubling problems.

Courses in this section of the curriculum deal with growth and development from infancy through adolescence and young adulthood to old age; there will be help in identifying various aspects of emotional disorder and some of the influences that have contributed to its development. There is continuous drawing on insights developed in such other professions as medicine and psychoanalysis and in philosophical and sociocultural discoveries.

Physicians, psychiatrists, and social scientists equipped to deal with the influences of sociocultural factors on human growth and personality development will probably participate with the social work faculty in the presentation of basic theory and in discussion of case materials.

Social Work Practice

This part of the curriculum has to do with teaching particular methods in social work practice; the most widely used and most quickly identified are case work, group work, and community organization. They are methods that have been developed to carry out social work's aims and tasks. Differences among them come primarily in relation to the type of problem to be met, the way in which people seeking help approach the social agency, the array of particular skills called for, and diversities in the settings and arrangements that have been developed for handling problems and giving service.

Their common roots in the philosophy, scientific knowledge, and disciplined approach to serving human beings, characteristic of social work, are receiving strong emphasis today. Social workers with developed skills in the use of one method of practice are working side by side with those using skills in another; essential skills and "ways of doing" of one method are being found to be transferable and enriching to the practice of a worker who may be using, primarily, the skills of another. In other words, it is *practice as a social worker* that is of supreme importance and the major concern of the professional school. Any separatist approach to selection of a particular concentration in practice can only be self-defeating.

The oldest established method in social work is *case work*. This calls for a person-to-person approach to helping individuals and families who are having difficulty in meeting problems in their day-to-day living. In methods courses and field instruction, the student will learn how to relate to his client in helpful and releasing ways and how to get at the roots of problems that may arise from within the personality of the individual seeking help or from tangled relationships that seem beyond his power to unravel; conflicts and pressures within his immediate environment may be the cause of the trouble. Whatever the nature of the problem or need, the student will learn to diagnose it carefully and to find and use resources available for giving help.

Because descriptions of a professional method of work almost inevitably tend to sound a bit formal, it may help to think of case work in its extraordinarily human aspects, and examples come readily to mind: helping Mrs. Young to find a lovable little girl underneath the exasperating patterns of rebellion and running away that have made her Denise such a problem at home and in school; finding a place for Jane Howard to await the birth of her baby, who will have no legal claim to a father's name; or helping ambitious Mrs. Smith to understand that her Robert, who is having difficulty at school, is not "dumb," but pressured by fears that get in the way of his reading. Securing remedial reading aid for Robert and working with Mrs. Smith to help her understand how her own drives may have entered into her small son's problem belong in case work. It is working with the Powells to fit together the positive pieces in their marriage, and it is standing by lonely, frightened old Mr. Flinn while trying to get an exact picture of his needs for sustenance, housing, or medical care.

Learning the art of relating warmly and of listening with ears that hear, eyes that observe, and a trained mind that can both elicit the real meaning of what it learns and weigh possible ways of moving to help are at the heart of this method of working with people. The art of sensitive interviewing and the ability to record accurately observations and interpretations of situations are central skills.

The *group work* method, as the term suggests, is concentrated on helping people, at all age levels, to meet their personal and social needs through their participation in group activities and in the experience of group relationships.

The important central learning here is the professional use of the group process. The group worker must learn not only to relate warmly to the group as a whole and to its individual members, but to so influence the group's life and activities that both they and the relationships of the group members to one another will contribute, to the utmost, to individual growth and well-being. Groups differ as individuals do, and the group worker will be under the necessity of learning how to study a group, to gauge its strengths and weaknesses, to interpret its history, and to predict the quality of indigenous leadership it is likely to develop. A group's capacity for self-government, self-control, and initiative in assuming a responsible place in the agency and in relation to other groups in the community are important areas for study.

The learning group worker is taught to be aware of the ways in which a group mirrors the environment from which its members come. Personal, social, and economic problems in living are not parked at the door of the clubroom, to be picked up again when the members leave; they come in with them, and their pressures are seen in the conflicts that arise between members and between groups.

The group worker learns to listen and observe. Actually, he has a unique and very useful vantage point, for over and beyond his face-to-face contacts with an individual with special needs, he is able to observe this member, not only in relationship to himself or with members of his family, but in relationships with his peers. In this relatively freer setting, where the member does not feel particularly under observation, his behavior can often be seen as a direct acting out of his individual drives or personal problems. The worker has to learn to interpret what he sees and hears if he is to use it soundly in determining his own activity in serving a group and its members.

And into what human situations his eyes and ears take him! He learns to intervene quietly on behalf of Joey, an undersized, frail little boy hanging on the periphery of an active boys' club. With little initiative or capacity for participation in the swift-moving life of the group, Joey is usually by himself, "drawing things" with bright crayons. The group worker's spoken comment on his drawing skill ("Joey can go to work on that ugly screen, and some of you fellows can help him") or a quiet suggestion that Joey accompany another boy to get permission for the group's use of a picnic site turns over a new and exciting page for Joey. His unbelieving, "Who? Me! I can't talk," reveals a damagingly low level of self-esteem; but a real feeling of belonging and being counted on can change this and it did! Joey came importantly to the next meeting with his own thought-out suggestions for a new name for the club.

Group work methods involve learning—often not too easily—to handle the necessary limiting of members' destructive activities, perhaps to protect the integrity of the group as a whole, perhaps to divert a potentially cruel singling out for ridicule or attack. It means learning how to reject behavior without rejecting its perpetrators and how to accept rejection by a group or individual without, in turn, rejecting.

It means learning, too, how to work with self-centered Mrs. Stern, encouraging her to find the status and response she so sorely needs, through participation in the doings of the Oldsters Club, and how to maintain a balance, always, in a group of older members, between concern for the many individual problems of impaired health, loneliness, and financial need and constructive group activities—perhaps in music or handcraft or discussion of national and world issues.

Always before the learning group worker is the need for close contact with a community, its rich resources for creative group programs, and its services for people with special needs; it may mean tapping resources for medical treatment, a chance to learn a trade or return to school, or coaching in English, perhaps, for members of a gang breaking up and feeling ostracized and without roots.

All of this means that methods courses in group work and related instruction in the field work agency are geared to helping the student understand the complexities and dynamics of group life, to assess the particular needs that bring individuals into group associations, and to find the root causes of problems that emerge within the groups.

Programs of social service, whether directed to helping people on a one-by-one or on a group basis, call for some form of overall organizational planning. When this need reaches beyond the activity of a single social agency to a total community, in which many agencies are at work in programs of social welfare, there is need for planning and co-ordination of effort on a community-wide basis. Students preparing for this area of practice will be in courses and field placements designed to develop their skills in *community organization*. Their courses will deal with how to help a community identify and describe clearly its social welfare problems and needs; how to coordinate the programs of agencies already at work; how to institute action to meet new or inadequately met needs and uncover the resources available for getting work underway. The financial support of social welfare activities is a matter of great importance, and there will be a focus of attention on ways of financing—particularly those of the United Fund, a method characteristic of so many American communities today.

Such activities do not remove the community organizer from working with people, and at professional school he will need to call into use all he is learning about the reactions and behavior of people, in order to understand and work constructively with groups, frequently of very different points of view. The purposes of one group of citizens ready to get on with a planning job may be blocked by the maneuvering of another when considerations of self-interest act as blinders to human needs. Out of a welter of suspicion and perhaps prejudice, fears of becoming too deeply involved, implusiveness and withdrawal of individuals, eagerness to get going and sitting on the fence, the community organizer must learn to use skills in bringing differences into solution. He must learn to find and use sound alternative ways of moving if earlier ones must be discarded; he may need to bring in new and challenging evidence of a given problem or to weigh a slowing up here in order to achieve needed advance there.

He is constantly observing and listening to a community in its strivings, and in company with his fellow case workers and group workers, he must be able to interpret soundly what he sees and hears as a basis for determining his own activity as a social worker and for predicting the direction groups may take. He is dealing at close range with the organized structure of a community and with citizens engaged in increasing the well-being of all its people.

In addition to acquiring skill in working with individuals, he must understand the dynamics of groups and, like the group worker, must learn to work creatively with a variety of groups. That they are organized primarily to do a job on behalf of the needs of others, rather than for their own enjoyment, growth, and development, does not alter the fact that they are groups made up of individuals whose concerns, interests, and ways of thinking and acting become basic areas of study for the community organizer.

All social workers, whatever their particular area of practice, will be called upon in the day-by-day doing of a job to carry through certain activities that are directly related to the administrative structure of the agency in which they work. One thinks quickly of all that is involved, for any worker, in program planning and coordination, in public relations, in keeping careful records, not only of individual professional activity but of statistical material needed to establish his agency's accountability—financial and otherwise. Many social workers are involved in the training and supervision of nonprofessional staff. These aspects of responsibility enter, where appropriate, into all the areas of practice courses.

There may be in the student body a small group approaching study in these areas on a total agency basis. The student here is usually a person with broad knowledge of social welfare goals, programs, and methods, and he usually has substantial experience in one or more areas of direct service. His practice study in *administration in social work* is usually arranged on an individual basis; it will take account of what is involved in turning policy into useful services to people needing them and of how to institute, in an agency, constructive management procedures, sound budgeting provisions, and enlightened personnel practices.

Over and above the learning and exercise in study and

research required of every social work student, whatever his chosen area of practice, schools are currently developing, at a fairly rapid rate, programs of study for the student preparing to practice more intensively in the area of *social work research*.

Here, too, it is usually true that such a student presents in his preprofessional activities some aspects of work and educational experience that have already established a focus of interest in and a degree of facility with research methods.

Social work research is aimed primarily at defining why certain services become a "must" for some people in a community, how agencies operate, the methods of practice they employ, and the ways of measuring their effectiveness. The student with a focus in this area is helped to select and draw on knowledge from related fields, particularly from the social sciences. An important emphasis is continually held before him; namely, he is not engaged in research in the ether, as it were, or for its own sake. His activity will always be tied up with some problem of identified concern to social work, and his objective, in common with that of his fellow students, is the development of services appropriate to the actual needs of human beings and of the communities in which they live.

There will be an opportunity in Chapter Seven to see these methods in use, at somewhat closer range, and to get a still broader picture of the elements that must enter the course content prescribed for each method as it is developed in classroom and in field instruction agency.

Meanwhile they should be drawn together in a prospective social worker's thinking as he contemplates their common significance and status in a professional school.

It is in the school's curriculum devoted to practice that the differences between academic study alone and professional education emerge most clearly. The professional school emphasizes constantly that, under its auspices, knowledge is being pursued not for its own sake but for immediate use in working with people and, through such service, for the production of identifiable values for society as a whole.

While the specific content in the various areas of practice will differ, students will be exposed to common approaches in the teaching of practice and will learn in the same basic ways.

The case records used in teaching bring the real world into the classroom, and the real, nonacademic situations into which assignments in the field instruction agency take him will bring the professional school student into close and vivid relationship with living men, women, and children—with people in trouble or struggling under the weight of needs that far outrun the possibility of immediate fulfillment; of hope running out; of lowered self-esteem and loss of belief in themselves; of sharply curtailed opportunity faced by young people for free and normal growth, for health and education, and for those experiences that make for expansion in place of imprisonment of the spirit.

A common thread running through all practice methods is the worker's constant responsibility for problem-solving. The professional student learning to undertake this responsibility will find a high degree of likeness in approach in all the methods being taught. Outlined, it would go something like this:

> What are the facts in the particular problem situation? What are the feelings of the people immediately involved about the problem, and how do they relate to other people in the situation?
> What do these factors spell out as the nature of the problem? If, on exploration, more than one difficulty is apparent, which appears to be the most crucial and why? In other words, should some priorities be set as to what to deal with first?
> What resources are available for meeting parts of the problem—within the individual himself or the group itself? Within the social agency and the skills of the worker? Within the neighborhood or the total community—city, town, county, state, or nation? What are the best ways of eliciting cooperation in each instance?

After exploration and diagnosis, the way that promises the best solution of the problem or of some of its parts must be selected, and resources appropriate to the particular needs in the situation must be used.

Study of results must follow, to estimate possible need for modification in the way selected and to take the next steps.

It is the element of judgment throughout this procedure that characterizes it as a professional approach.

Field Instruction

There have been many references to field instruction as an important part of the educational program of the professional school. Because it may be the least familiar means of learning to the student whose undergraduate education has been largely concentrated in the classroom, there should be some further comment on its place and significance in the total program.

Every student's program of study will include spending an appreciable amount of time working in a social agency, where, under the guidance and tutelage of a professionally trained member of its staff, he will carry out specific assignments. Most schools plan for field placement within the regular "in-residence" school period, that is, concurrently with the classroom program; several schools arrange their field experience on a block plan, providing for the student to be absent from the school for blocks of time devoted to fieldwork in an agency.

In the simultaneous arrangements, approximately one-third to one-half of the number of semester hours required for the degree will be spent in the field. Placements usually last for one academic year. Placement for the second year is usually in another agency, to encourage breadth of experience and increased professional capacity.

One has only to think of educational procedures employed in preparing for other professions—internship for the doctor, practice in briefing for the lawyer, pastoral assignments for the student for the ministry—to understand the importance of this practice instruction in schools devoted to professional education for social work.

It will be well, at the outset, for the student to see this particular aspect of training as an integral part of his whole program. The social agencies used for student instruction are very carefully selected for their suitability as settings for an educational experience. The staff member to whom the student is directly assigned is chosen on the basis not only of his competence as a social worker, but of his ability as a teacher, for he must impart and share knowledge and encourage the development of social work skills in the student's direct contact with individual clients, groups and their members, or with total communities.

These teaching social workers are very important to the school; they are usually called *field instructors*, indicating their role as definitely an educational one as part of the teaching staff of the school. In his field placement, therefore, the student is every bit as much "in school" as he would be in classroom or university library. The social agency is a living organism, and it is here, as he begins to practice his profession in a program of help to real people, that the student will learn to put his expanding knowledge to use and to sense the satisfaction of his growing skills in the art of relating to and working creatively with people.

As an incoming student you would undoubtedly be full of questions and speculation about what is expected of you in your fieldwork placement. When your school adviser talks this over with you, you will be encouraged to speak about your major interests and what your experience to date has meant to you. There will be a serious attempt, then, to match these and indications of your educational needs with the learning opportunities a given agency and instructor can provide.

On the first day in the agency, you would meet and talk with your instructor; a careful plan of orientation would introduce you to the agency staff and provide you with immediately needed information about the agency's program of services, as well as its most routine procedures and the whereabouts of its facilities and resources.

There is usually eagerness, if some trepidation, to get to

work on actual assignments. These are usually determined in consultation with the school adviser. For one student, there would be the assignment of specific individual cases—the number and nature somewhat dependent on the student's experience; for another, there would be the assignment of groups with which he would work throughout the academic year, and for still another, specific responsibilities in a program of community organization. This might involve working with a particular committee, assisting in the exploration of a needed service, or securing information needed for a piece of work in the planning stage.

For all students there are planned experiences to acquaint them with the day-by-day activities of a social worker. These might include attendance at a meeting of a local community council or a conference of workers; sitting in on a group consultation with a psychiatrist; holding intake interviews with parents about camps for their children; or visiting day-care centers used by the agency. Students in fieldwork usually attend agency staff meetings and sometimes board and committee meetings.

As the time approaches for a first interview with a client or the first meeting with a group, your instructor will be ready to discuss your plans with you and interpret the records you may have been reading to get you abreast of what has been happening before you take over.

The instructor is always accessible; but there will also be a regular schedule of one-and-a-half to two-hour conferences weekly. The student worker is expected to submit to the instructor, prior to this conference, written records of his activity in interviews or group meetings, committee meetings or other assigned responsibilities. This record forms a basis for discussion and gives the instructor leads for the future direction of his teaching.

It is a most important tool for your learning, too, because it helps you to analyze the situation you are working in and to assess your own activity in it. It also provides the material for further diagnosis and planning. As experience grows, you are encouraged to move and act more and more independently, and the content of your weekly conferences with your instructor will reach higher levels of learning on your part and teaching on his.

It is an exciting and in many ways a reassuring experience to take a responsible place in a busy agency and to learn to know and work directly with its clientele of real people in an accountable way. You are working in a real world of problem and need; each day's work brings the vivid colors of actuality into class discussion or reading of relevant theory.

Professional Attitudes and Disciplines

Aspects of learning in the professional school that cannot be pinned down neatly within the syllabus of a given course or within any one specific experience in the field agency or within the pages of any book in the library are the more subtly acquired understandings that build the self-disciplines of the professionally educated social worker. These understandings will be fed from many springs during the two years in school, and the student who is not overfearful of change within himself will find himself freer and surer in relationships with people and readier to accept the disciplines that develop both competence and artistry in performance.

Of first importance is that, along with absorbing knowledge and developing skills in working with people, the student will use every opportunity in his total program of professional education to gain understanding of his own attitudes and reactions and clarity as to their possible impact on the relationships through which he is seeking to help others. Unlike the pure scientist, who in dealing with his materials is largely outside of them, the scientist in social relations is inside the situation with the people he is seeking to help. His reactions and attitudes are an important element in the relationship through which the problem is being approached. Professional education provides the means and encouragement for learning how to deal with one's subjective feelings and personal modes of reaction so that they will not stand in the way of an objective approach to any situation; such an approach allows for an unhampered use of knowledge and learned skills, free from the encroachment of personal biases or unexamined modes of reacting to people and situations.

This growth in self-awareness and self-discipline is one of the most significant aspects of learning in a program of professional education. It distinguishes the trained social worker from one without training; it begets the confidence of members of the other professions and disciplines—doctors, lawyers, teachers—with whose professional practice the social worker will be in constant touch. Most important of all is the self-trust it generates and the freedom it gives to devote precious energy to the validation, through practice, of the motivation for serving others that brought the student into social work in the first place.

The need for this professional quality and the everyday opportunities for its expression in practice are implicit in the specific career opportunities presented in the job descriptive material of Chapter Seven.

6

A Career in Social Work

Although social work is one of the youngest of the helping professions, its knowledge and skills are now being brought to bear on the problems and needs of millions of Americans in communities all across the United States, and there is a strong crescendo in the demand for more and more workers.

Social welfare today has been referred to as "big business," and there is justification for the term in the fact that as a nation we spend annually more than five billion dollars on governmental and private welfare services (this figure does not include amounts expended from the social insurance programs under the Social Security Act).

It is estimated that some hundred and five thousand social welfare workers are on the job today, translating these billions into direct services to people.* When a career in social work is being considered, however, that is not the whole story; the demand is for *trained workers,* for whom there are three times as many jobs open as there are qualified workers to fill them. There is an estimated need for upwards of fifteen thousand additional trained workers each year, just to hold the present line of opportunity for service.

* *Salaries and Working Conditions of Social Welfare Manpower in 1960,* a survey conducted by the Bureau of Labor Statistics, in cooperation with the National Social Welfare Assembly, 345 East 45th Street, New York 17, N.Y.

Salary Levels and Job Security

With plenty of jobs available, social work can also be cited as a profession offering a sound degree of financial security. With striking gains between 1950 and 1960, its salaries are still moving steadily upward. In the light of rapidly developing needs and opportunities for trained workers, this trend, together with the steady increase in numbers of jobs available, is likely to continue for a long time.

Without doubt, the increasing entrance of men into this field of work has helped to boost the salary scales, and this can be expected to continue. Social work is no longer considered, as it once was, largely a women's profession.

Group work and community organization especially offer many job opportunities for men. Their numbers are growing, too, in child welfare and child adoption agencies. In the correctional field and in institutions of various kinds, the need for trained men social workers is great, and the number employed is steadily increasing.

On the basis of 1961 figures, the salaries of men and women with professional education and experience qualifying them for senior staff and supervisory positions range up to $8,000 a year and over. Administrative positions may pay from $10,000 to $25,000. The more highly paid administrative jobs are in federal and state programs and in national or large local voluntary organizations.

It is more difficult to estimate average pay levels for the beginner, but it can be said with assurance that every new social work school graduate, even if his experience is the minimum required for the degree, can expect to consider four or more jobs, generally at a starting salary of between $5,200 and $6,000. From this it will be seen that salaries of social workers at all levels of experience and responsibility tend to parallel similar grade-level salaries of ministers, teachers, nurses, and librarians.

Different sections of the country will show some diversity in salary ranges, and those quoted here may move somewhat up or down in line with these local differences.

One note of caution in our consideration of earnings in social work: while its beginning salaries compare well with
those in the other professions, and advances come steadily
with increased responsibility, the top-level salaries in this profession are earned by men and women in full-time jobs—usually as administrators—and should not be compared with the
fees—often on a "what the traffic will bear" basis—paid to
such professionals as doctors and lawyers operating independently. Large fees for consultant or other professional services
should not be looked for in social work. Instead, we must
look for the compensating factors.

In contrast to professions in which promotions are slow
and arduous, social work, with its persistent personnel short-
ages, promotes its qualified people very rapidly. This current
fluidity in the field brings both financial and job status rewards in its train. Because in social work specialization is recognized but not too rigidly treated, its workers are less apt
to be frozen in one type of job or one kind of setting. Once
the basic professional qualifications are secured, its workers
are able either to move up from one level or kind of practice
to another in a given agency or to move out and across the
line from one type of agency to another and from one kind
of job to another.

Such mobility holds particular value for married women
workers. With a social work degree, a woman need have few
compunctions about moving to wherever her husband's work
takes him. If she wishes to continue to work professionally
after marriage, there will be a social work job for her almost
anywhere. Further, a trained woman worker who gives up
her career when she marries can count on being able to return
to the field in a professional capacity after her family is established.

Working Conditions

Generally speaking, working conditions and personnel
standards are good in the field of social work, and they are
improving where need for betterment shows up.

Faced both with the obligation to apply to their personnel, as well as to their clients, beliefs about the essential worth and rights of people and with the very practical pressures imposed by shortage and mobility of workers, agencies study their personnel codes and practices and introduce steadily rising standards. Normal provisions are for regular annual salary increases, sick leaves, paid annual vacations—usually longer than in many occupations—and participation in medical and hospital insurance.

In most of the governmental programs of social welfare, civil service guarantees of tenure and promotion apply; in addition to coverage by social security, many agencies have some form of retirement benefits.

Studies have been made, and will undoubtedly continue, to get at what constitutes an equitable work load for workers of varying degrees of experience and in different types of jobs. Uniformity, even if desirable, would be difficult to reach because of the differences in what will be occupying the case worker, group worker, or community organizer in a given space of time. Preparation for and the conduct of interviews with individual clients, home visits, arrangements for taking a child to a foster home, or consultation with a psychiatrist cannot easily be compared with what a group worker will have to be doing at the same time to get ready for a group meeting at the center or for a group's excursion or for a block of time away from the center for investigation of the trouble that broke out on Avenue X last night. Days may pass for the community organizer with no specific meetings, but he may be deeply involved in interviews with individual community leaders, drawing up formal proposals, or making a direct exploration of a neighborhood or agency situation.

The very nature of a social work job usually precludes rigid nine-to-five daily schedules; but controls are usually set to keep the work week within a thirty-five- to forty-hour total and to assure, at regular intervals, two consecutive and uninterrupted days of rest and relaxation.

These comments apply to the profession as a whole. In the

next chapter, we shall look at some of the work opportunities available in more specific day-by-day terms before returning to further, and final, discussion of the "fors" and "againsts" that should enter into serious consideration of social work as a professional career.

7

Fields of Practice

Where and into what kind of job does the trained social worker go?

As we know, social workers are employed in many settings, helping people of all ages—from the very young to the very old—with a wide range of troubling human problems or unmet needs.

The specific job may be within a tax-supported governmental welfare service or in a privately supported social agency. Variety in job opportunity prevails within both.

Case Work Practice

Where service to people, individually or as members of a family unit, is the major characteristic of the agency's program, there will be employment opportunities primarily for social workers whose practice study has emphasized the *social case work method.*

PUBLIC ASSISTANCE

A major opportunity for case workers is in the public assistance programs of state, county, and municipal departments of welfare. In these departments, services are devoted to giving assistance to families and individuals who are without sufficient money to maintain themselves.

In any day's work within these governmental programs, the social worker may be working with people temporarily out of a job and without funds to bridge the gap in earnings, with widows and dependent children, with the blind, and with men and women who because of permanent disability are unable to meet their own financial needs. The applicant will often be a lonely old man or woman, long past the age of capacity to earn a living, and very possibly needing, in addition, both a place to live and medical care.

Whatever the basis of need, all these situations will call for the utmost in compassion and gentle and sensitive handling. As the social worker explains the legal provisions for establishing a client's eligibility for one or another form of financial assistance, it is expected that he will always seek to protect the applicant's dignity and the maintenance of his self-respect at this time of needed outside help. Along with assisting people with their applications and determining their eligibility for financial assistance, there will be need for encouraging them to find and make use of their own capacities to work through some of their immediate problems. It may be necessary to turn to specific resources in the community for legal aid for a client or to a vocational testing or employment service on his behalf. Needed appliances for a physical disability may have to be secured, or a family may have to be directed to a neighborhood center for recreational activities, possibly including a trip for some of its members to summer camp.

All such activity must be carried out with the constant and steady aim of helping those seeking assistance to move toward self-maintenance and independence. Primary learned skills in the art of listening and of establishing a warm and helpful relationship are absolutely essential.

The public assistance worker, in the nature of most of the jobs, should be a graduate of a school of social work. Under existing conditions of stringent personnel shortage—peculiarly pressing in all forms of public welfare service—this is not generally true. The program is of colossal size, and the number of jobs far outruns the supply of trained workers to fill them. Still, studies reveal a steady increase in the number of trained workers in the direct service jobs in public welfare; and, as might be expected, these are the workers who move into this agency's special jobs of analysis, staff training, supervision, and other administrative responsibilities. An increasing number of state and city departments are providing—particularly for their rank and file workers—leaves for study and financial grants to enable them to secure professional education.

Every state has a public welfare department, usually in the state capital. Further information can be obtained from such an office. Beginning jobs that do not require professional training frequently include those of investigators, case aides, or home visitors.

When we turn to work with families and individuals in the private agency, we are looking at one of the oldest and most highly respected forms of social work in this country.

FAMILY CASE WORK

Most communities of ten thousand people or more have a family service agency. As the term suggest, the focus is on the family and its relationships, and highly skilled professional service is directed to both prevention and solution of problems that threaten the stability of the family. Where the troubled individual is part of a family group, the case worker is usually involved in services to the family as a whole; an individual, wholly detached from family, receives services based on his individual needs.

Day by day the case worker may be listening to and counseling with a couple whose marriage seems moving toward breakup, or may be helping to get to the bottom of serious conflicts between children and their parents. Frictions arising in the community from the influx of increasing numbers of neighbors of different racial or cultural background or from relations with landlords charged with racial bias or blamed for unsafe and pitifully inadequate homes may be the threatening factor. Immediate problems due to the presence in the family of a physically or mentally handicapped member or a neglected child may require solution.

Whatever the situation, the worker helps those involved to understand the causes of the problem and encourages them to find and use the resources they have within themselves for meeting it; at the same time, he will be utilizing, as needed and appropriate, outside resources for rebuilding the damaged family situation. There is no magic formula here; people's problems can be as complicated as people themselves, and each situation will call for skillful and discriminating help.

In these jobs, the worker will often have occasion to consult specially equipped persons in other professional fields and authorities—medicine, psychiatry, legal aid, the ministry, vocational guidance resources, housing authorities, and home economics facilities, for example.

CHILD WELFARE

Both the public and the private agency, interested in the protection and strengthening of family life, carry a very special concern for children and the forces that may prey in damaging fashion on their young lives. There are challenging and very rewarding jobs in their special services to children.

Child welfare, in a general sense, includes all those social and economic goals the agencies adopt and the programs they put in motion for ensuring, to the highest degree possible, the healthy growth and normal development of the individual child.

Child welfare services supplement and sometimes substitute for parental care of children. The children brought or referred to the agencies may be handicapped in their development by physical, mental, or emotional problems; they may be suffering from acute neglect or actual abuse. At a given time, young children may present a heavy load of worry to the mother who must leave the home every day to earn a living. For varied and sometimes multiple reasons, children get into trouble with the law and need protective help. Children born out of wedlock or who come from broken homes or homes where death has removed one or both parents may be in situations of particular need.

What may the child welfare worker be called on to do in these instances? With no attempt at being exhaustive, these are some of the activities that may occupy him in the course of a day.

Because a primary aim is the maintenance of stable family life, he may be seeking, through counseling with them, to strengthen and extend the parents' own efforts to provide a healthy environment for their children's development. Some situations, however, will call for solution outside the natural family setting, which may indeed not exist or may at the moment be actually damaging to the child.

When, after careful exploration, it is seen to be necessary, a foster home or a place for institutionalized care may have to be found. Relief for an overburdened working mother and protection of her young children may involve finding suitable day-care services, or the services of a visiting homemaker may be needed if the mother is ill.

Use of community resources will be a constant activity for this worker, especially where help may be needed for a child with a hearing or speech difficulty or any other handicap that may be crippling his chances for normal growth.

What can happen to children in the years when they are least able to fend for themselves can beggar the imagination of the lay person learning about acute problems for the first time. For example, there are such horrors as the chaining of tiny children to a table or chair for periods when parents are absent, severe beating of children by their parents, and babies being bitten by rats in buildings no longer fit to be lived in. Such stories occasionally get into the daily papers, and variations of them will come to the child welfare worker. So too will the more subtle instances of damage to children from overpressuring by parents, use of a child as an emotional weapon by fighting parents, or denial of the child's need for association with others his own age.

The child welfare worker carries a heavy responsibility on behalf of any community that cares about its children. As he uses his professional knowledge and skills in dealing with family and community conditions that hurt children, as he selects a foster home for a child and provides continued counseling to foster parents, and as he works directly with the child in ways that assure him that he is cared for and that nurture the growth of his own individuality, this worker is making a contribution that reaches far into the future.

Some communities, aroused to the need, have established special child guidance clinics, extending services of a concentrated kind to children where personality damage has already gone deep and whose behavior problems are beyond the capacity of parents to deal with alone. The problem is even more complicated when the parents themselves are unable to help because of their own emotional difficulties. A member of the audience which recently witnessed a performance of the half-hour play *Boys at Large*, under the joint auspices of the Police Precinct Youth Councils of New York City and Plays for Living, said at the end, "Children aren't half as confused as their parents are."

The social worker in these situations is usually equipped with advanced psychiatric knowledge and treatment experience. He must be particularly skilled at working in close collaboration with a psychiatrist and probably a clinical psychologist in carrying out individually planned treatment programs.

Similar services are made possible in detention centers for children, in corrective institutions for the treatment of emotionally disturbed children, and in hospitals.

School Social Work

A rapidly developing field for the social worker with case work knowledge and skills is that of school social work. It follows rather naturally on modern education's emphasis on the individual child and his development that the doors of many schools have been thrown open to workers with social work training.

The school social worker acts as a liaison between the school, with its teachers, and the homes and neighborhoods from which the children come. It is not difficult to see that a child's problems in school may have their roots in unsatisfactory conditions and poor relationships in his home or in frightening and damaging pressures in his immediate neighborhood.

The school social worker works continuously with individual children to help them make needed adjustments. The efforts of the teachers to help children make the best use of their learning opportunities are supplemented and furthered by the social worker who is dealing constantly with overtimid or withdrawn children or with children whose problems drive them into aggressive and noncooperative behavior, into truancy and running away. Neglect, undernourishment, or lack of normal affection in the home may be found to be the major causes of the problems of children whose reaction to what bothers them gets acted out in the classroom.

In such situations, the daily tasks of the school social worker will take him into relationships with other resources for helping—particularly those within the school itself: the teachers, the school doctor or nurse, the psychologist, and others. Outside the school, this social worker will be in touch with organized groups that effect the life of the child and with the social agencies whose resources can be called upon for help.

The school social worker, who must be a warm and caring person, can forge strong links of support for the child himself, between him and his family, and between his family and the school. He can help the child to find and use the resources in the community that are a part of his rightful heritage.

Case workers working primarily with families and individuals in trouble or need will be found in many agencies in the community. In addition to those that have been described here in some detail, they will be working in similar situations within the home service departments of the Red Cross and the Salvation Army, in the more specialized and more transient services of the Traveler's Aid, and in case work and special services departments of settlement houses and community centers, whose major area of service is in group work.

It remains to speak of work opportunities in three other

types of service that call primarily for case work knowledge and skills: medical social work, psychiatric social work, and social work in the correctional field.

MEDICAL SOCIAL WORK

Medical social work includes social services given in hospitals, clinics, and other health facilities. It has developed with the growing emphasis in medical care on the need to see treatment of a patient in terms of wholeness, to include attention to the social and emotional factors as well as the physical factors in illness.

What might a medical social worker be doing in any typical day in the social service department of a hospital or clinic? Without question she will be using her knowledge and skills to help patients, and quite often their families, with problems that either are emotional or are in the area of practical needs that tend to arise where illness is a central factor. She may be helping a patient and his family to understand more clearly and cooperate more fully with medical recommendations or to use after-care facilities in the community.

The medical social worker is, characteristically, a member of a team that includes the doctor, the nurse, and possibly other professional personnel who have a hand in ensuring care for the individual patient. The doctor may call on the medical social worker for information about the patient's home situation and his ways of adjusting, meaningful for his own understanding and treatment of the illness.

Schools of medicine make use of medical social workers in their teaching faculties to participate in the training of nurses and public health personnel. These social workers will also be found on the staffs of community health service agencies.

There is a serious shortage of professionally educated personnel in medical social work.

PSYCHIATRIC SOCIAL WORK

Psychiatric social work presupposes a direct relationship with the scientific knowledge and the healing skills of psychiatry. The psychiatric social worker may be at work in a mental hospital or other residential treatment institution or clinic. Here, too, the social worker will be an important member of a team concentrating on programs of individual treatment; teams will include psychiatrists, physicians, nurses, and possibly occupational therapists. The social worker will carry responsibility for interpreting the patient's background and family relationships to such a group.

With the patient himself, there will be continuous opportunity for encouraging positive response to treatment; with the family, there may be a chance to foster deeper understanding of the nature of the illness and of the desirable adjustments to be made in the patient's interest. There may be further need to help patients and their families with particular adjustments when the patient returns to his home.

In the child guidance clinics, the psychiatric social worker draws into a positive working relationship the patient and his family, clinic personnel and community resources. She may be assigned, too, to work with the psychiatrist in treating a child and/or the adults in his family.

Social workers who have the necessary professional preparation in this area may, upon graduation from professional school and in connection with their own military service, serve as officers in the U.S. Army and U.S. Air Force, where they will work in close association with army doctors and psychiatrists. They may possibly conduct intake interviews with servicemen who have shown symptoms of mental or emotional disturbance and carry out some of the provisions involved in the disposition of cases that call for contact with the serviceman's family or securing treatment facilities in a hospital or his home community.

Like medical social workers, psychiatric social workers may participate in the training of other personnel working in programs of mental health and rehabilitation.

There is a rapid increase in the expenditure of government funds for establishing and expanding mental health services, and the demand for psychiatric social workers in community programs for prevention, diagnosis, and treatment is steadily growing.

CASE WORK FOR THE COURTS

From its earliest beginnings, social work has shown a deep concern for people who have run foul of the law. Our national forum on the concerns of social work—the National Conference on Social Welfare—was, at its inception in 1873, named the National Conference on Charities and *Corrections!* (The present name testifies to progression in thinking to the more positive and universal term of "social welfare" to cover all varieties of social need and problems that press in on people and all the programs designed to give help.)

There is increasing cooperation between social workers and the police and courts responsible for arrest and the imposing of legal sentence. The psychological insights that have themselves revolutionized social work's ways of giving service, whatever the area of problem or need, have shown clearly that the controls of authority can go only so far in the correction of human behavior. When, within the boundaries of whatever sentence and controls the court imposes, provision is made for a relationship with a social worker who will help the offender recognize the areas in which he still has scope to move on his own account, the rehabilitative objectives of corrections are being introduced. These include finding and encouraging the use of opportunities the defendant has for exercising some freedom, for making the decisions that are still his to make—about school, job, medical treatment, or group associations. He must be helped to face realistically and accept responsibility for whatever he has done and to share in efforts to find solutions for the problems that have been found to contribute to his difficulties.

There is a growing movement toward adoption of these rehabilitative methods by the courts, and with it has come an increasing demand for the professional social work skills that make them possible. The settings for this service are the juvenile court, domestic relations and criminal courts, and the temporary detention homes and correctional institutions for children, adolescents, and adults. About nine thousand probation and parole officers are working directly with individuals either placed on probation without prison sentence or paroled into community life before the expiration of their prison terms.

As in the relation of the medical or psychiatric social worker to the physician, the social worker in the correctional field carries responsibility for providing the court with accurate information about the background and person of the offender and the social situation within which the offense was committed. This information is taken as one element in the material assembled as a basis for the court's judgment and recommendations. When probation is prescribed, the social worker–probation officer takes up his responsibility in the name of the court and on its behalf.

Day by day in such a job, the social worker acts as one who must maintain, on behalf of the court and society, a surveillance role, but also as one who carries into that responsibility a warm, friendly interest with which he will help the probationer establish some goals for what he wants to do with his life, determine constructive steps for reaching these goals, and develop the potentialities he possesses for positive attitudes and behavior as a responsible citizen.

Opportunities in these more specialized areas of case work practice are limited for beginning, inexperienced workers. Social workers in these positions have very often taken additional training in postgraduate courses in professional school or have interned after school in settings that provided for intensive learning under highly professional direction. A firm foundation in basic case work method is an essential first step.

Group Work Practice

We turn now from practice which is carried on primarily in a one-to-one relationship between social worker and client to practice in which the worker will be using his social work knowledge and skills to guide group activities, member participation, and intermember relationships in social agencies where work with voluntary groups is the primary method of service.

Such groups—so characteristic of our culture—are organized or sought by people of all ages for their strong social values of warmth of companionship, identity and status in belonging, and the opportunity they afford for enlarging interests and for exciting new experience.

Examination of such groups—usually made up of people of like age and interests—leaves no question as to the potency of the influence they can exert over their individual members. It is recognized that this group power may, depending on setting and internal leadership, operate for socially destructive as well as for positive ends of individual and group enrichment.

The group worker is aware of individual needs and aspirations at different age levels and recognizes the effect on personality of physical, social, or psychological deprivation. He understands the individual's deep need for recognition, for the feeling of belonging, and for doing things with close companions. Because he knows that a guided, positive group experience can provide these values in ways not possible in solitariness, he uses his skills to make a group's life and activity meet these needs, help temper the personal stresses of its members, and encourage their normal growth and social adjustment.

Where do such social workers "hang their hats"? And what might one expect to find them doing in any day's work?

They are employed in community centers under public or private auspices; in social settlements and weekday program centers of churches; in the local branches or chapters of such national youth-serving agencies as the YMCA and YWCA, Jewish Community Centers and Catholic Youth Organizations, Boy and Girl Scouts, Camp Fire Girls, Boys and Girls Clubs; and in day and country camps maintained by any of the above or under separate but noncommercial auspices.

When working directly with a group, our social worker will be helping its members work and play together in ways that promote mutual understanding and sound relationships; they may be groups of children, adolescents—in or out of gangs—young adults, parents, or old people.

He will be helping such groups develop their own leader-

ship and carry responsibility for their own affairs, in democratic ways and in an atmosphere of freedom and mutuality
among members. Because conflict is a natural element in and
between groups, the social worker's sensitive understanding
and skill will be called for continuously in helping groups
resolve those conflicts that can bring serious hurt to members
or inject fear or hatred into relationships between groups.

He will be engaged in helping groups plan program activities which are satisfying and recreative and which stimulate
members to venture into broadening areas of knowledge and
into deeper appreciation of our common heritage in all aspects
of man's creativity.

Uncovering need—particularly that deepened by deprivation in living—and finding and using the available resources
for meeting it are day-by-day activities of the social worker
in these settings. His knowledge of his community's resources
must be comprehensive, and his skills in making them accessible to people, ready and disciplined. Here the need may be
to find just the right physician to provide sound sex education for an adolescent group. Or the worker may open up
opportunities for visits, for meeting significant people, or for
actual participation in community projects. Such projects
might be for developing better feeling between racial groups
or for cleaning up an open park or play area. The scope of
program interest is well-nigh inexhaustible, and the imagination and creativity of this social worker will be in constant
use.

He may be working individually with a child whose needs
and drives are so pressing as to lead him into behavior in a
group that brings down on him the disapproval of his fellow
members and sometimes hurting pressures to be more con-
forming. Such a youngster's individual problems may be so
deep that, until they can be brought into solution, his attempts to participate in the hurly-burly of a group may not
bring him the help he needs in self-understanding and the
adjustments his situation calls for; his referral to individual
case work service within the center, or to a child welfare
worker in another agency, may be occupying the group

worker. The disciplines connected with such referrals call
for deep knowledge and skill and sensitivity in their use. The
same qualifications and quality of understanding would be
needed where an older member of the community center
needed financial assistance, a place to live, or medical attention.

STREET CLUB WORKERS

Our group work social worker may be using a settlement
or community center as a base, but also working alone out
on the dark corners and rubble-cluttered empty lots of a city's
streets. Here he works patiently and knowledgeably to make
contact with gangs of preadolescent and adolescent boys and
girls whose deprivations and deep-seated suspicions of the social center keep them outside its doors. On their own, they
often move into antisocial and destructive activities, into organized conflict with other groups like their own—con-
tenders for their staked-out territories—and, tragically, into
violent warfare and bloodshed.

In several large cities, municipal and state governments,
aroused by a startling rise in juvenile delinquency, are working with private agencies to put increased numbers of trained
social workers into the streets of especially affected neighborhoods. It is a demanding and frequently lonely job; it can be
a frustrating one, too, in the slowness with which small gains
can be made. Beginnings in building confidence, extending
needed services to individuals and their families, and instituting some positive program features wherever the groups for-
gather can be swiftly cut across by a new outbreak of open
violence, with a resulting need to begin again the whole slow
building process.

Gains may not be spectacular, but they are meaningful and
rewarding when they come in situations that are challenging
so many of our American communities.

GROUP WORK IN SPECIAL SETTINGS

In addition to the usual settings, social workers whose
practice study has emphasized the social group work method

will be found in such special settings as hospitals, rehabilitative centers, and guidance clinics, in corrective institutions for children and adults, and in camps and centers organized to meet the needs of handicapped persons.

Here, as in the case of the medical or psychiatric social worker, the group worker becomes a member of a treatment team, and the central object of service is always the individual. The knowledge and skills the group worker brings will be used, however, in organizing informal groups, in the belief that the values of group relationships, however tenuous and short-lived, and of group activities can contribute importantly to individual treatment. Knowledge of the community and the home from which the patient or client comes and to which he will return is a contribution this worker makes to the team's understanding. Within the groups organized, the worker will, through program activities and group discussion, help the members get ready for discharge and return to home communities. The tempo of group activity in these settings is slower; its goals must be set in relation to carefully estimated degrees of individual capacity and within the requirements of collaboration with the other members of the team. These disciplines are demanding, but they bring satisfaction to the workers who are answering a steadily increasing call for social workers with their particular knowledge of group experience and its potential contribution to individual adjustment, together with the trained ability to use it creatively.

Most of the agencies that employ professionally trained group workers also have part-time workers—volunteer and paid—in certain phases of their program. The job of the trained worker often includes responsibility for recruiting, training, and supervising some members of the nonprofessional staff.

The need for trained workers in all the settings that demand group work knowledge and skills is crucial. A person whose career interest is in this direction will find jobs plentiful and the opportunities they offer insistent and challenging.

Community Organization Practice

There is a fairly recent but quite rapidly moving trend in the professional schools to make more systematic provision for students seeking practice study opportunities that emphasize methods of professional community leadership that will prepare them for a variety of jobs as *community organizers*.

The longest established and best known of these jobs are those related to United Funds. More than two thousand American communities now use this plan for supporting and financing social welfare services. Trained social workers will also be found in Community Chest organizations and in such coordinating agencies as community welfare councils or councils of social agencies.

The more demanding jobs here, involving direction of a division or department, call for substantial experience. Many people holding them have already demonstrated ability in the use of other basic social work methods. There are, however, increasing opportunities for less experienced workers as assistants to chest or council executives, where their responsibilities may include assignments in the organization of educational or financial campaigns, working in public relations or community planning, or research work as a part of program planning.

In day-by-day working terms, this often means working with a community group to increase the number of day-care centers for children or old people or to discourage duplication of services by agencies in the neighborhood. The group may plan a campaign for increased play space or a campaign to get housing authorities to include recreation space in new developments or permit more tenant participation in planning.

Differences in viewpoint must be expected, but helping the people involved to find common objectives and to work steadily toward them is a challenging and engaging occupation. In interviews or in conferences with community leaders from a variety of backgrounds—industry, organized labor, professional groups, and citizens' groups—there are occasions to interpret the aims of social welfare programs in their various forms and the kinds of services they make possible.

In communities that are making efforts to combat problems of delinquency, trained social workers with skills in community organization are being called into jobs where their home base may be either a strategically located settlement house or community center or the office of an organization coordinating the efforts of many agencies and community institutions and establishing special neighborhood programs to combat this serious problem.

These social workers may be busy exploring needs and turning up flagrant aspects of social conditions that breed delinquency and crime. The workers will maintain relations with churches and schools, with departments of governmental services, including public housing, welfare administration, public employment service, police, and the courts. Some community organization specialists may be initiating new services; for example, training and employment service for the thousands of unskilled school dropouts who, each year, swell the numbers of potentially delinquent adolescents. They may be employed by one of the city's own bureaus and be working directly in, say, tenant organizations aimed at strengthening morale and well-being in units of public housing.

Private agencies, too, especially those with strong influence in their surrounding communities and concern for the causes of human problems, are looking for workers with special abilities in community organization. Here the worker may be doing administrative work and social planning—perhaps interpreting his agency's programs of service to the community, or charting ways for the agency to move toward changes in its social policy, or recommending ways in which it should participate in community programs.

Social Work Research

Many of the programs described, and increasingly those of private agencies of high professional standards, are being built on the findings of controlled research; and graduates of the professional schools who have not only interest and a certain flair, but sound training in research methods are finding stimulating and satisfying opportunities in various areas of social work research.

This type of research can be expected to make important contributions to the further establishment of social work as a profession; it should help in further clarification of its aims, enrich its body of knowledge, and give direction to what it will teach in its professional schools. It will undergird the leadership role social work must assume in interpreting to society as a whole and to any community in particular the underlying conditions that will lead to human degradation and what needs to be undertaken to ensure a standard of human well-being commensurate with economic and material achievements. Interest, ability, and substantial work in advanced courses in the school are necessary to equip a worker for employment in this field.

Social Work Abroad

Young people interested in the possibility of a career in social work frequently ask about opportunities to work in other countries.

In common with some of the jobs just described, the demand is chiefly for workers whose competence and experience are already well established. Many of the new nations are rapidly instituting programs of social welfare along with their programs for economic development. The professional schools of social work in this country enroll, each year, many students from other countries who will return to take up important jobs at home. (At this time, more social workers from abroad have studied in the United States than in any other country.)

But, in addition, as the nations come closer together for mutual helpfulness and interpretation of need, opportunities develop for the use of American-born and -trained social workers of proven ability to work abroad. They are called upon to establish social welfare services, often in close cooperation with a foreign government or with units of work established by the United Nations or by national organizations in the United States whose international programs include sending American workers abroad. In short, activities in international social work are carried on by the United Nations, by national governments, including that of the United States, and by many nongovernmental agencies with international programs of service.

Looking to the Future

As experimentation with new ways of meeting human problems continues, variations and combinations of responsibility occur in many of the job opportunities described in these pages. The field is a broad one, the problems tenacious and challenging, and the needs of people caught in them go very deep.

Why do men and women choose to work in jobs like these, in situations of such compelling urgency and complexity? What are the rewards that transcend the considerable investment in time and money required for professional education? What, in face of the unceasing demand for the use of precious energy in putting knowledge and skill to work in imaginative, creative, and disciplined fashion, can make each day's work an exciting and satisfying adventure?

The next and final chapter attempts to answer some of these questions and will give some consideration, too, to other sides of social work—some of its possible drawback areas that certainly should be given thought and careful weighing in a career decision.

Every such individual decision has important implications both for the person making it and for social work, where the need is profound for workers who, from conviction and spirit of dedication to its purposes, will provide the leadership to carry it into widening areas of usefulness and a place of deepening significance among our country's helping professions.

8

Rewards and Some Hurdles— but Definitely a Future

Answers to the questions posed at the end of the last chapter are, in large measure, implicit in the questions themselves.

These social work jobs will provide:

Continuous opportunity, with the excitement that goes with it, for using one's deepest knowledge and creative powers in situations of urgency and complexity. There will be weariness, yes—but very rarely boredom!

Close association with people and the wonder and deep stirring that come with never-ending discoveries of gallantry of spirit and of human capacity and potentiality for growth and change. Sorely tried and bodily weary Mrs. A.'s quiet, "I think I can do it," or physically handicapped Jimmy's, "Look! See! I'm walking!" or a group member's, "Let him go first; I can wait," will tell you about this.

Deep satisfaction that comes from helping individuals and groups to recognize and use their own reserves of strength and creativity and from making resources available to help them do so. It is such a simple thing to say that everybody should have the opportunity to develop to his full potentiality—but social workers know the barriers that block the way for so many. They know, too, the deep privilege that is theirs in possessing knowledge and skill that can help open doors—real doors—to jobs, to health, to release from crushing financial anxiety—and that can help open doors of the spirit, too, through encouraging a fellow human being to trust his own ability. The words may be simply, "Remember? You were able to do that—you can do this, too," but the assurance is, "People do care," and, "You are not alone."

An active sense of being needed and of contributing to helping a community meet its obligations to its citizenry. Every newspaper item that says, "More social workers are needed in this program," tells us not only that jobs will be available but that groups in the community recognize the contribution social workers can make and know why they are needed.

Discovery that social work is a "stuff-of-life" profession, dealing intimately with people in their infinite variety. Human problems and needs may show likenesses, but people are unique, and no mechanical or bag-of-tricks way of dealing with their concerns will suffice.

Growing conviction that, in working with people, the best will never be good enough. This conviction, in turn, provides a strong incentive to increase knowledge and skill and to achieve more and more expertness and artistry in their use.

Close association with fellow workers who feel about this as you do. In entering this profession, you join a goodly company of men and women; they will share your concerns and give stimulus to your thinking and planning as you meet with them in the staff of your own agency, in local chapters of the National Association of Social Workers, in its national assemblies, in meetings called by the Council on Social Work Education, in the National Conference on Social Welfare, and in other seminars and conferences that bring social workers together.

Close association, too, with members of other professions.

Day-to-day work with doctors and nurses, teachers, lawyers, judges, clergymen—all dedicated, in their own professional fields of service, to the advancement of the common good— is often part of a social worker's job. The feeling of being an essential part of this "one-direction" tide of effort to increase human well-being brings its own reward, so that a social work career affords not only a means of making a living but a way of making a life.

But Are There No Shadows?

No hurdles to meet, no frustrations to block this road of opportunity and promise? Of course there are! No vital job is without them. Has any "bed-of-roses" job ever really met the spirit's full desires? And even roses have their thorns.

What are some of the particular thorns in the social work job?

One that comes quickly to mind is the possibility of impatience and even irritation on the part of social workers when, along with increasing demand for social work services, there persists in sections of the same community a hazy and often thoroughly distorted public image of the social worker on his job.

There are different facets to this distorted image. It may represent a vestigial carry-over from an earlier day, when uninformed attitudes toward the bases of human need tended to vitiate the manner of giving service and to discredit such basically ennobling human impulses as "living in charity, one with another" and "doing good." The stereotype of the do-gooder, with whatever connotations it carries from the past, has undoubtedly taken on additional and more subtle coloring from attitudes held by many people in the midst of today's developments in the field of social welfare.

Social work comes closer than some of the professions to upsetting other distorted but quite jealously held images— views that many individuals hold of themselves and views of society held collectively by sections of it. Fantastic developments in business and industry, created through man's initiative, are countered by increasing numbers of disrupted lives. The fact is that concern for human values and protection of the individual's well-being do not always keep pace with advances in economic competition and preoccupation with material productivity.

Lack of knowledge, ability, or inclination to wrestle with this situation will continue to lead some of our fellow citizens to find comfort in now largely disproven ideas about the origins of human need and problem. Some will continue to believe that these problems are inevitable and must always be with us and should not get too much attention; others will contend that they should not exist in a time of prosperity and that when they do they signify only weakness on the part of the individual affected—a lack of capacity, on his part, to meet the expectation that any "upstanding American" can always get a job, support a family, and cope with whatever life brings.

It is not too long a step from this thinking to the creation of cruel stereotypes of problem-bewildered people as "weaklings" or "parasites" and of the social worker—administering a program of service that challenges these premises—as a "coddler" or an "extravagant spender of the public's dollars." Some of this reasoning frequently blocks an individual's approach to his own problems. Resistance to seeking help because that conflicts with an image of self-sufficiency often deepens the problem itself and denies him access to help.

Even without these stereotypes, old-fashioned notions about social work persist. One of these is that its services are limited to providing something called "charity" to the indigent; and the flavor of the term "charity," so used, is far removed from its warm, selfless, and life-giving original meaning. This conception fails to grasp how complex and interacting the situations of human problem can be, and it shows little or no understanding of the skilled services social workers are called upon to give.

Social workers have access to steadily increasing knowledge

about the effect on human functioning of both the lack and
the overpressuring of human relationships. They know how
the stresses of modern life—including both financial and
emotional insecurity—can destroy perspective, distort reality,
and undermine capacity to absorb and adjust; their knowledge
runs far ahead of popular understanding and of general willingness to accept that these are areas of human breakdown and
illness that can strike at all income and cultural levels and
bring hazards to total communities. The help provided by a
social worker must be based on deep knowledge of the origins
of such illness and distress, familiarity with and access to ways
of treatment, and sound methods for eliminating their underlying social and economic causes.

In contrast with those of the more established professions,
the services given by social workers take on a certain quality
of anonymity. The teacher and the priest, rabbi, or pastor,
have an established status and place of honor and respect in
our culture; and although distressing, it is quite respectable
to be physically ill, and to call the doctor is an accepted procedure. On the other hand to be having difficulty in intimate
family relationships or to be unable to handle a situation of
financial need through thrift and independence is, in our
culture, beyond the pale for many people. The masses of people needing and receiving help of all kinds are, in the nature
of the case, the least articulate in any collective effort at interpretation of services, and much of social work goes un-
recognized and unsung!

The press may headline a community's social problems and
call for their redress but, with some exceptions, will not help
public understanding of what those "needed" social workers
will actually do. Social work, in spite of its phenomenal advance as a profession, is not a common newspaper headliner,
and the individual social worker, very much engrossed in his
or her day-by-day business, may never appear there.

It helps to remember that the older professions have met
and weathered similar distortions in popular understanding.
There are very encouraging signs, too, that the interpretive
efforts of community leaders, of the press, of writers of fic-

tion and drama, and of those responsible for our common channels of communication are turning the tide on behalf of better understanding of social work. It will continue to be true that the social worker's own day-by-day demonstrations will provide the most essential interpretation of what social work is about.

The effects of these distortions will differ from worker to worker and will shift, too, with changes in the immediate situation. In a day of disappointment over unfulfilled hopes —either personal or those for a client—the blow will seem heavier, and a good old attack of futility in a job "nobody understands" may get you down. It is even harder to take when these attitudes turn up in a worker's own family, with Uncle B. booming that he "never thought a niece of mine would get mixed up with such doings" and possibly Aunt C. adding a negative note of anxiety about "what you might catch in those dirty slums."

There is comfort in the fact that feelings about such attitudes usually evaporate quickly, for the job itself brings resilience to the spirit. But the would-be social worker needs to remember that he will be vulnerable to such attacks.

Another question that may be raised is about a seeming slowness in many of social work's ways of dealing with problems. We mentioned earlier the street worker in a tough neighborhood whose weeks of work in gaining contact with those he is seeking to help, slowly building up a relationship of trust through which to extend further service, may seem to go for nothing when a sudden outbreak of gang violence cuts across his efforts and the pieces must be picked up and the process begin again. There are many less dramatic instances when the case worker's efforts to get at facts in a situation, to untangle badly twisted relationships, to separate the real from the fancied—to deal sensitively with areas of deep reticence or with continuing return to old ways of acting even when the possibilities of new ones have been glimpsed —may seem to spell progress only by inches—and with difficulty, often, in identifying the inches.

It will be helpful to think of all professions in connection with this concern, for it is a point at which they meet. In social work, we think of it as the place where the precision of a knowledge-guided scientific approach merges with the needed artistry in its application, and we say "needed" artistry because the elements involved are the experiences, and feelings about them, of human beings.

A good many years ago, Dr. Richard C. Cabot * warned social workers—and, indeed, most professional people in America—against a temptation to work "in a hurry." Recognizing that professional work is never finished and that the end of each day finds much more left to do, he saw us in danger of equating the need to do all we can with an obligation to do it at top speed. But Dr. Cabot reminds us that "first-rate work is almost never done in a hurry."

Social work has come to underscore the validity of this counsel, as its own developments have given emphasis to the importance of quiet concentration to find the true core of a problem, of steadiness and sensitivity in relation to the feelings of people under stress, of patience to help them find and use their own resources of strength, and of leaving no stone unturned to make accessible whatever resources of help the agency and the community provide.

People will differ in their ability to work in this way and to await results that are sometimes very slow in coming. It is in no spirit of disparagement that it is suggested that social work may not be the career for the person with a low tolerance of deferred achievement and a need to check things off on a "done" list.

When attention is directed to the vast areas of the still undone in social welfare, still other questions plague the social worker. In face of such crying need and of the countless thousands of troubled people who never reach the sources of help, does the little we can do really matter? Isn't ours a "drop-in-the-bucket" approach? In the article just referred to, Dr. Cabot writes, "Everyone, then, who attempts work of a professional grade is leaving untouched endless vistas of work

---

* Richard C. Cabot, "Ethics and Social Work," published in *The Survey*, vol. 56, April–September, 1926.

that he might accomplish were he not a finite being." Dr. Cabot felt that this should not be a counsel of despair, but one of hope; he reminded us that "the work of the world is infinite, and we are finite, but no man or woman is intended to do or to attempt the work of the world—only to do a fair slice of it *in such a way* as to stimulate others to do their slices." *

The radius of the influence of our efforts and of the methods we use will reach out beyond measurable limits. This does not make it a comfortable occupation, but it is one in which faith in the capacities of the people we work with—clientele, fellow workers, and an enlightened public—and confidence in ourselves and our professional tools will bring deep rewards if we grasp the truth that while "unable to visualize infinity, every one of us deals with it every day." **

Concern for the "vast undone" will receive some of its severest jolts on specific occasions when the "powers-that-be" seem blind to opportunities for expanding services and moving to find the material ways and means to make that expansion possible.

The "powers-that-be" may be the board of your own agency or the budget committee of the community's United Fund; it may be a seemingly recalcitrant group in state or federal government or a department of municipal government which refuses action that would modify current policy, enlarge present programs, or provide appropriations for new forms of service.

As professional workers and citizens, we live and work within a democratic frame of reference, and decisions that are important for the concerns we feel strongly about are in the hands of those whom "we the people" elect to represent us. Characteristically, in a free society, our institutional provisions—public and private—will not move evenly or always consistently. More vision at one point will be encountered by apparent apathy or even seeming regression at another.

* *Ibid.*
** *Ibid.*

But Again, the Direction
Is Unmistakable

There is no turning back the clock. Social work faces a huge task as it deals with needs that are still inadequately met and with new ones that will inevitably accompany the accelerated pace of social change in this country.

In her presidential address to the National Conference of Social Work of 1940, Dr. Grace L. Coyle said, "We remember the Dark Ages into which the exhausted energies of men have sunk back to despair and brutishness. But we must remember that that is not all of history. Throughout its course those who have achieved the beginnings of social justice, who have freed the human intelligence, who have set the humane against the brutal passions of men, have moved forward in a fragile and wavering advance. But they have moved forward. The rise of science, the achievement of political democracy, the abolition of slavery, the extension of medical care, the free education of the young, and the development of that vast body of social services which we represent—these are but part of that struggle for a civilized life. Our generation is called upon to hold this line and to press forward. This struggle is the great adventure of mankind, faltering, broken, uncertain, but with it all, superb." *

The prospect today is for still greater participation by our government in the business of human welfare, as well as for intelligent experimentation by the private social agencies. This is where social workers must stand up and be counted. They have both knowledge and experience to bring to bear, as their day-by-day activity enters into the fabric of a democratic society; their leadership can give direction and a quickening of pace to needed areas of social action if they remain true both to their own roots and heritage in the American tradi-

---

* Grace L. Coyle, "Social Work at the Turn of the Decade," *Proceedings of the National Conference of Social Work,* Columbia University Press, New York, 1940.

tion and to the insights and disciplined understandings they have acquired along the way.

In the closing pages of his book *Social Work in the American Tradition,** Dr. Nathan Cohen says, "The story of Social Work in America is a reflection of our faith in democracy not only as a form of government but as a way of life. It is the story of people and how they fare as the nation grows, develops and changes. Social Work, therefore, is predicated on faith in the average man, in his ability to govern himself and to handle his rights and responsibilities maturely. It recognizes the potentialities of man regardless of race, creed or national origin. It approaches him in terms, not of what he is but of what he can become if given equal opportunity and if dealt with justly. It further recognizes that man does not exist apart from his social relationships, and that in an increasingly inter-dependent society he has not only rights but also responsibilities to other men and their cooperative undertakings. Social work makes its best contribution as it regards its professional knowledge and skill, not as ends in themselves, but rather as means to an end, a better life for all mankind."

For some workers, there will be difficulties because the profession is so young and so imperfect. Are the bases on which we build practice really valid? So little seems proved scientifically. Isn't there still too great dependence on trial-and-error approaches? Aren't we given to hasty and frenzied clutching at something believed to represent the latest mode of "good," but actually largely untested and unproven? We ought to know more! And, here, the more experienced the social worker, the more fervent will be the "Amen."

This is why the new recruits to the profession are welcomed so eagerly by those already at work, for they see in the new generation the leadership that must carry the profession of social work to new levels of knowledge and attainment. Social workers today continue to experience the stimu-

---

* Nathan E. Cohen, *Social Work in the American Tradition,* The Dryden Press, Inc., New York, 1958. Quoted by permission of Holt, Rinehart and Winston, Inc.

lation and excitement of ground-floor building of a profession, and there is no hesitation in their invitation to join. Convinced that the raw edges in social work are also its growing edges, the opportunity they extend so eagerly is that of growing with a profession, inside it, and with boundless opportunity for making direct contribution to its developing wisdom, insights, and skills.

These workers promise more—not overtly, but in being the kind of people they are. Without fanfare, new members of the profession give recognition and deep acclaim to the support gained from social workers on the job, who continue to work selflessly, productively, and with imagination—within limitations of public policy and agency settings and in the midst of the baffling complexities of human need—without loss of values and with strong retention of faith in their profession.

Very significant people have gone this way.

Appendix

The National Commission for Social Work Careers, 345 E. 46th
  St., New York 17, N.Y.
  (Jointly sponsored by the Council on Social Work Education
  and the National Association of Social Workers.)
                        and
The National Association of Social Workers, Inc., 2 Park Avenue,
  New York, 16, N.Y.
  The addresses of local chapters of the NASW will be found
  in the telephone directories in a great many communities across
  the country.
Council on Social Work Education, 345 E. 46th St., New York
  17, N.Y.
National Social Welfare Assembly, 345 East 46th Street, New
  York 17, N.Y.
  Lists bibliography of materials on social work.

Local Social Work Recruiting Committees
  Promote summer work experience in social work for college
  students.
  Careers in Social Work: Room 700, 123 West Madison Street,
  Chicago 2, Illinois.
  Careers Program: Community Welfare Council of Buffalo and
  Erie County, 921 Genesee Building, Buffalo 2, N.Y. California
  State Program for Social Work Careers: State Dept. of Social
  Welfare, 2415 First Ave., Sacramento, Calif.
  Valley Regional Program for Social Work Careers: Dept. of
  Mental Hygiene, 1500 Fifth St., Sacramento, Calif. Bay Area

Program for Social Work Careers: Bay Area Welfare Planning Federation: 577 14th St., Room 415, Oakland, Calif.

Social Work Careers Program: 3 Walnut Street, Boston 8, Mass.

Social Work Recruiting Center of Greater New York: 105 East 22nd Street, New York 10, N.Y.

Careers Department, Council of Social Agencies of Rochester and Erie County: 70 North Water Street, Rochester 4, N.Y.

Careers in Social Work: 2400 Reading Road, Cincinnati 2, Ohio.

Careers in Social Work: % The Welfare Federation, 1001 Huron Road, Cleveland 15, Ohio.

Careers in Social Work: Room 420 Suburban Station Building, Philadelphia 3, Pa.

Careers in Social Work: % Health and Welfare Association of Allegheny County, 200 Ross St., Pittsburgh 19, Pa.

Commission for Social Work Careers, Los Angeles Region Welfare Planning Council: 731 So. Hope St., Los Angeles, Calif.

(*Note:* Local health and welfare associations, welfare federations, or councils of social agencies can also be turned to for information.)

NASW Code of Ethics

(Adopted by the Delegate Assembly of the National Association of Social Workers, October 13, 1960) *

Social work is based on humanitarian, democratic ideals. Professional social workers are dedicated to service for the welfare of mankind; to the disciplined use of a recognized body of knowledge about human beings and their interactions; and to the marshaling of community resources to promote the well-being of all without discrimination.

Social work practice is a public trust that requires of its practitioners integrity, compassion, belief in the dignity and worth of human beings, respect for individual differences, a commitment to service, and a dedication to truth. It requires mastery of a body of knowledge and skill gained through professional education

* Reprinted here with permission of the National Association of Social Workers, from *NASW News,* vol. 6, no. 2 (February, 1961).

and experience. It requires also recognition of the limitations of present knowledge and skill and of the services we are now equipped to give. The end sought is the performance of a service with integrity and competence.

Each member of the profession carries responsibility to maintain and improve social work service; constantly to examine, use, and increase the knowledge upon which practice and social policy are based; and to develop further the philosophy and skills of the profession.

This Code of Ethics embodies certain standards of behavior for the social worker in his professional relationships with those he serves, with his colleagues, with his employing agency, with other professions, and with the community. In abiding by the code, the social worker views his obligations in a wide context as the situation requires, takes all of the principles into consideration, and chooses a course of action consistent with the code's spirit and intent.

As a member of the National Association of Social Workers I commit myself to conduct my professional relationships in accord with the code and subscribe to the following statements:

I regard as my primary obligation the welfare of the individual or group served which includes action for improving social conditions.

I give precedence to my professional responsibility over my personal interests.

I hold myself responsible for the quality and extent of the service I perform.

I respect the privacy of the people I serve.

I use in a responsible manner information gained in professional relationships.

I treat with respect the findings, views, and actions of colleagues, and use appropriate channels to express judgment on these matters.

I practice social work within the recognized knowledge and competence of the profession.

I recognize my professional responsibility to add my ideas and findings to the body of social work knowledge and practice.

I accept responsibility to help protect the community against unethical practice by any individuals or organizations engaged in social welfare activities.

I stand ready to give appropriate professional service in public emergencies.

I distinguish clearly, in public, between my statements and actions as an individual and as a representative of an organization.

I support the principle that professional practice requires professional education.

I accept responsibility for working toward the creation and maintenance of conditions within agencies which enable social workers to conduct themselves in keeping with this code.

I contribute my knowledge, skills, and support to programs of human welfare.

Graduate Professional Schools
of Social Work
in Canada and the United States

(Accredited by Commission on Accreditation, Council on Social Work Education)

All schools of social work provide a two-year sequence of class and field instruction in the method of social case work; a number of schools (marked with a *) provide a similar sequence in the method of social group work. Some schools provide opportunities for related class and field instruction in community organization, in administration, and in research.

For identification purposes, schools offering third-year and doctoral programs, or both, are marked with the †.

UNITED STATES

CALIFORNIA

*† University of California, School of Social Welfare, Berkeley 4, California

University of California at Los Angeles, School of Social Welfare, Los Angeles 24, California

*† University of Southern California, School of Social Work, Los Angeles 7, California

COLORADO
  * University of Denver, The Graduate School of Social Work, Denver 10, Colorado

CONNECTICUT
  * University of Connecticut, School of Social Work, 1380 Asylum Avenue, Hartford 5, Connecticut

DISTRICT OF COLUMBIA
  *† The Catholic University of America, The National Catholic School of Social Service, Washington 17, D.C.
  * Howard University, School of Social Work, Washington 1, D.C.

FLORIDA
  Florida State University, School of Social Welfare, Graduate Program in Social Work, Tallahassee, Florida

GEORGIA
  * Atlanta University School of Social Work, Atlanta, Georgia

HAWAII
  * University of Hawaii, School of Social Work, Honolulu 14, Hawaii

ILLINOIS
  *† University of Chicago, School of Social Service Administration, Chicago 37, Illinois
  * University of Illinois, The Jane Addams Graduate School of Social Work, Urbana, Illinois
  Chicago Branch, University of Illinois, 833 South Wood Street, Chicago 12, Illinois
  Loyola University, School of Social Work, 820 North Michigan Avenue, Chicago 11, Illinois

INDIANA
  * Indiana University, Division of Social Service, 122 East Michigan Street, Indianapolis 4, Indiana

IOWA
  State University of Iowa, School of Social Work, Iowa City, Iowa

KANSAS
  * University of Kansas, Graduate Department of Social Work, Kansas City, Kansas

KENTUCKY

University of Louisville, The Raymond A. Kent School of Social Work, Louisville 8, Kentucky

LOUISIANA

Louisiana State University, School of Social Welfare, Baton Rouge 3, Louisiana

*† Tulane University, School of Social Work, New Orleans 18, Louisiana

MARYLAND

University of Maryland, School of Social Work, 721 West Redwood St., Baltimore, Maryland

MASSACHUSETTS

Boston College, School of Social Work, 126 Newbury Street, Boston 16, Massachusetts

* Boston University, School of Social Work, 264 Bay State Road, Boston 15, Massachusetts

Simmons College, School of Social Work, 51 Commonwealth Avenue, Boston 16, Massachusetts

† Smith College School for Social Work, Northampton, Massachusetts

MICHIGAN

Michigan State University (College of Social Science), School of Social Work, East Lansing, Michigan

*† University of Michigan, School of Social Work, Ann Arbor, Michigan

† Wayne State University, School of Social Work, Detroit 2, Michigan

MINNESOTA

*† University of Minnesota, School of Social Work, Minneapolis 14, Minnesota

MISSOURI

University of Missouri, School of Social Work, Columbia, Missouri

Saint Louis University, School of Social Service, 3801 West Pine Boulevard, St. Louis 8, Missouri

*† Washington University, The George Warren Brown School of Social Work, St. Louis 30, Missouri

NEBRASKA

* University of Nebraska, Graduate School of Social Work, Lincoln 8, Nebraska

New Jersey

* Rutgers, The State University, Graduate School of Social Work, New Brunswick, New Jersey

New York

* Adelphi University, School of Social Work, Garden City, Long Island, New York

State University of New York at Buffalo, School of Social Work, 19 Library Circle, Buffalo 14, New York

Columbia University School of Social Work, 2 E. 91st St., New York 28, N.Y.

* Fordham University, School of Social Service, 134 East 39th Street, New York 16, New York

* Hunter College of The City University of New York, School of Social Work, 695 Park Avenue, New York 21, New York

* New York University, Graduate School of Social Work, Washington Square, New York 3, New York

* Syracuse University, School of Social Work, 926 So. Crouse Avenue, Syracuse, New York

* Yeshiva University, Wurzweller School of Social Work, 110 West 57th Street, New York 19, New York

North Carolina

University of North Carolina, The School of Social Work, Chapel Hill, North Carolina

Ohio

*† Ohio State University, School of Social Work, Graduate Program, Columbus 10, Ohio

Cincinnati Center of Ohio State University, University of Cincinnati, 206 Teachers College Building, Cincinnati 21, Ohio

*† Western Reserve University, School of Applied Social Sciences, Cleveland 6, Ohio

Oklahoma

University of Oklahoma, School of Social Work, Norman, Oklahoma

Pennsylvania

† Bryn Mawr College, Carola Woerishoffer Graduate Department of Social Work and Social Research, Bryn Mawr, Pennsylvania

*† University of Pennsylvania, School of Social Work, 2410 Pine Street, Philadelphia 3, Pennsylvania

*† University of Pittsburgh, Graduate School of Social Work, Pittsburgh 13, Pennsylvania

PUERTO RICO
* University of Puerto Rico, School of Social Work, Rio Piedras, Puerto Rico

TENNESSEE
* The University of Tennessee, School of Social Work, 8810 Broadway, Nashville 3, Tennessee
Knoxville Branch, The University of Tennessee, P.O. Box 8820, University Station, Knoxville, Tennessee

TEXAS
* Our Lady of the Lake College, The Worden School of Social Service, San Antonio 7, Texas
University of Texas, School of Social Work, Austin 12, Texas

UTAH
* University of Utah, Graduate School of Social Work, Salt Lake City 12, Utah

VIRGINIA
Richmond Professional Institute School of Social Work, 800 West Franklin Street, Richmond 20, Virginia
Norfolk Branch, Norfolk College of William and Mary, Hampton Boulevard and Bolling Avenue, Norfolk 8, Virginia

WASHINGTON
* University of Washington, School of Social Work. Seattle 5, Washington

WEST VIRGINIA
West Virginia University, Department of Social Work, Morgantown, West Virginia

WISCONSIN
* University of Wisconsin, School of Social Work, Madison 6, Wisconsin
University of Wisconsin—Milwaukee, School of Social Work, 3203 North Downer Avenue, Milwaukee 11, Wisconsin

CANADA

BRITISH COLUMBIA
* University of British Columbia, School of Social Work, Vancouver 8, British Columbia

MANITOBA
* University of Manitoba, School of Social Work, Winnipeg, Manitoba

ONTARIO
University of Ottawa, School of Social Welfare, St. Patrick's College, Ottawa, Ontario
*† University of Toronto, School of Social Work, Toronto 5, Ontario

QUEBEC
Laval University, School of Social Work, Quebec, Quebec
* McGill University, School of Social Work, 3506 University Street, Montreal, 2, Quebec
Université de Montréal, L'Ecole de Service Social, C.P. 6128, Montréal, Quebec

Partial List of National Voluntary
Social Agencies
Employing Social Workers
in Their Local Chapters or Branches

American National Red Cross: 17th and D Streets, N.W., Washington 6, D.C.

B'nai B'rith Youth Organization: 1640 Rhode Island Avenue, N.W., Washington 6, D.C.

Boys' Clubs of America: 771 First Avenue, New York, 17, N.Y.

Boy Scouts of America, Inc.: National Council, New Brunswick, N.J.

Camp Fire Girls, Inc.: 65 Worth Street, New York 13, N.Y.

Child Welfare League of America, Inc.: 44 East 23rd Street, New York 10, N.Y.

Family Service Association of America, Inc.: 44 East 23rd Street, New York 10, N.Y.

Girls' Clubs of America, Inc.: 265 State Street, Springfield, Mass.

Girl Scouts of the U.S.A.: 830 Third Avenue, New York 22, N.Y.

National Board of the YWCA of the U.S.A.: 600 Lexington Avenue, New York 22, N.Y.

National Catholic Welfare Conference, Inc., Youth Department: 1312 Massachusetts Avenue, N.W., Washington 5, D.C.

National Council on Crime and Delinquency: 44 East 23rd Street, New York 10, N.Y.

National Council of the YMCA of the U.S.A.: 291 Broadway, New York 7, N.Y.

National Federation of Settlements and Neighborhood Centers: 226 West 47th Street, New York 36, N.Y.

National Jewish Welfare Board, Inc.: 145 East 32nd Street, New York 16, N.Y.

National Travelers Aid Association, Inc.: 44 East 23rd Street, New York 10, N.Y.

United Community Funds and Councils of America, Inc.: 345 East 46th Street, New York 17, N.Y.

Note: These agencies can be asked about full-time beginning jobs for college graduates, without professional education, who must work before entering professional school. State, county and city departments of public welfare may also be able to refer inquiries about such beginning jobs.